Politics
&
the Press

Politics

&

the Press

edited by RICHARD W. LEE

George Gallup, Jr.
David S. Broder
William Raspberry
William L. Rivers
Elmer E. Cornwell, Jr.
Otis Chandler
Philip Potter
Herbert G. Klein
Kurt and Gladys Lang
Irving Dilliard

 PUBLISHED BY **Acropolis Books** / WASHINGTON, D.C.

This book is the result of the "Distinguished Journalism Lecture Series," a project of the Department of Journalism, University of Maryland. The lectures were made possible by a grant from the A. S. Abell Company Foundation and the Baltimore Sunpapers.

Special gratitude is due to Mr. William F. Schmick, Jr., President of the A. S. Abell Company Foundation; Mr. Perry J. Bolton, Assistant to the President of the Foundation; and Mr. Philip Heisler, Managing Editor of the Baltimore Evening Sun, who were instrumental in getting the Lecture Series started.

The purpose of the Lecture Series and its subsequent book publication is to provide a forum for the expression of ideas by distinguished journalists and scholars of journalism, and to provide a continuing medium of education and exchange between the Journalism Department, its students and alumni, and the journalism profession.

CONTEMPORARY ISSUES IN JOURNALISM

Volume I : Politics and the Press
Volume II : The Crisis in Urban Communication

EDITORIAL BOARD

© *Copyright 1970, Department of Journalism, University of Maryland*

First Printing, May 1970
Second Printing, October 1970
Third Printing, August 1971
Fourth Printing, June 1972

ACROPOLIS BOOKS
*Colortone Building, 2400 17th St., N.W.
Washington, D.C. 20009*

Printed in the United States of America by
COLORTONE PRESS, Creative Graphics Inc.
Washington, D.C. 20009

*Type set in Bodoni and Futura Medium
by Colortone Typographic Division, Inc.*

Design by Design and Art Studio 2400, Inc.

Library of Congress Catalog Number 72-118670

Standard Book No. 87491-132-X (cloth)
87491-131-1 (paper)

CONTENTS

8 INTRODUCTION

13 ROLE OF THE PRESS IN PRESIDENTIAL POLITICS
by Elmer E. Cornwell, Jr., *Professor of Political Science,*
Brown University

35 APPRAISING PRESS COVERAGE OF POLITICS
by William L. Rivers, *Professor of Communication,*
Stanford University

57 POLITICIANS AND BIASED POLITICAL INFORMATION
by David S. Broder, *Political Columnist,*
The Washington Post

75 A PUBLISHER'S VIEW OF CREDIBILITY
by Otis Chandler, *Publisher, Los Angeles Times*

89 THE ADMINISTRATION'S VIEW OF PRESS AND POLITICS
by Herbert G. Klein, *Director of Communications,*
The White House

105 POLITICAL REPORTING: THE CRITERIA OF SELECTION
by Philip Potter, *Washington Bureau Chief,*
The Baltimore Sun

117 POLITICS, BLACKS, AND THE PRESS
by William Raspberry, *Columnist, The Washington Post*

129 THE INFLUENCE OF POLLING
ON POLITICS AND THE PRESS
by George Gallup, Jr., *President,*
American Institute of Public Opinion

145 TELEVISION DISTORTION IN POLITICAL REPORTING
by Kurt Lang, *Professor of Sociology,*
State University of New York,
and Gladys Lang, *Assistant Director,*
Center for Urban Education

169 POLITICS AND THE PRESS: A FINAL COMMENT
by Irving Dilliard, *Ferris Professor of Journalism,*
Princeton University

185 INDEX

I am opposed to censorship of television or the press in any form. I don't care whether censorship is imposed by government or whether it results from management in the choice and the presentation of the news by a little fraternity having similar social and political views. I am against censorship in all forms.

But a broader spectrum of national opinion should be represented among the commentators of the network news. Men who can articulate other points of view should be brought forward. . . .

I am not asking any immunity from criticism. That is the lot of the man in politics; we would have it no other way in this democratic society. But my political and journalistic adversaries sometimes seem to be asking something more— that I circumscribe my rhetorical freedom, while they place no restrictions on theirs.

We do not accept those terms . . . for continuing the national dialogue. The day when the network commentators and even gentlemen from the New York Times enjoyed a form of diplomatic immunity from comment and criticism of what they said—that day is over. . . .

—Vice President Spiro T. Agnew
November 20, 1969
Montgomery, Alabama

News media in this country also give a distorted picture. . . . I sometimes worry that the information media control the government. The so-called credibility gap is sometimes made bigger than it is because conflict is news.

—Vice President Hubert H. Humphrey
April 14, 1967
Athens, Georgia

Introduction

IN 1967, VICE PRESIDENT HUBERT HUM-
PHREY made a two-day political excursion to
Georgia to patch fences with Governor Lester Maddox. In an address to University of Georgia students
he dressed down a press that had given him poor
marks on a recent European tour, a tour that had
not been well received either at home or abroad.
The speech received little national attention.

Two years later, Vice President Spiro Agnew,
angered by a press critical of the Nixon Administration's speeches on Vietnam, bitterly criticized press
performance in speeches in Des Moines and Montgomery. These were well reported, indicating increasing national as well as media concern about the
relationship of press and politics.

Both men, frustrated by the forms their attempts at publicity had been given, questioned the
role of the press. It is equally well to question the
role of the politician in this relationship that is so essential to a democratic process where decisions are

made by informed voters. And, it is to the questions raised by this relationship that ten scholars and practitioners addressed themselves in the lecture series sponsored by the *Baltimore Sunpapers* and the Department of Journalism at the University of Maryland. It can be said at the outset that all of the answers are not here, but the discussions by the ten speakers are provocative and insightful. They cover a number of assigned facets and provide the student of politics and the press new ideas to explore and develop.

Several of the discussions bring to bear what is lacking in the remarks of both vice presidents—a necessity for the politician and for the press to understand the motivation of the other. In this area, three of the discussants—Professors Elmer Cornwell of Brown University and William Rivers of Stanford University and Mr. David Broder, *Washington Post* columnist—see the relationship as one of adversaries. The politician attempts to use the press to further his policies and goals; the press uses the politician to gain information necessary for the fulfillment of its task. Professor Cornwell examines the records of four national leaders—two American presidents and two British prime ministers—and the attempt of each to develop and use "image capital" to promote his programs. Professor Rivers finds both the press and the politician guilty of what he calls "inhibitions of the truth." These include the selective processes of journalists, the herd instinct of political reporting, and the continuing adversary relationship. Mr. Broder explains that the relationship of politician and press can be good or bad, tense or relaxed, smooth and workable, or angry and contentious—but it can never be neutral. In keeping with his assigned subject, Mr. Broder then goes on to discuss politicians' attempts to bias political news.

Los Angeles Times Publisher Otis Chandler addresses his remarks to the problems raised by declining press credibility, sensing the public disenchantment with media that was to become apparent in the public's agreement with Vice President Agnew's remarks. Herbert Klein, White House Director of Communications, discusses the mutual desire of administration and press to be credible and points to changes in the Nixon Administration that attempt to open the flow of information. The essay by Mr. Philip Potter, Washington Bureau Chief of the *Baltimore Sun*, explains the process of selecting the relevant political story and the small band of political reporters who cover "new acts and out-of-town openings" and are thus influential beyond their number in bringing new political figures into national attention. Mr. William Raspberry, columnist for *The Washington Post*, discusses the means by which the urban poor have found and commanded media attention.

Mr. George Gallup, Jr., and Professors Kurt and Gladys Lang present technological areas that have had a great influence on political affairs in the last twenty years. Mr. Gallup, president of the American Institute of Public Opinion, suggests that polls have become the "creative arm of the government" by discovering quickly the likely response to proposals, innovations, and laws. Professors Lang and Lang draw upon their experiences of twenty years of investigation of broadcast media to isolate some of the political phenomena of that medium and to make proposals for its improved use. Professor Irving Dilliard, Ferris Professor of Journalism at Princeton University, provides a concluding summary, pointing particularly to the weaknesses of present day political reporting.

The editor, as chairman of the 1969 Distinguished Lectures Committee, is grateful for the assistance of Professors Ray Eldon Hiebert and S. M. Vinocour, both committee members, and of Lee F. Coney and of my wife, Gail.

RICHARD W. LEE

College Park
January 1970

CHAPTER ONE

Role of the Press in Presidential Politics

by

Elmer E. Cornwell, Jr.

Professor and Department Chairman, Political Science
Brown University

PROFESSOR ELMER E. CORNWELL, JR., is a student of American politics and has concentrated upon the presidential use of the mass media in directing public opinion. He has been the chairman of the Department of Political Science at Brown University for the past eight years.

Professor Cornwell is the author of *Presidential Leadership of Public Opinion* as well as articles on the relationship of press and politics that have appeared in *Journalism Quarterly, Public Opinion Quarterly, Social Forces, The Midwest Journal of Political Science,* and the *Annals of the American Academy of Political and Social Science.*

He has participated practically in politics as an alternate delegate to the Democratic conventions of 1960 and 1964 and as the director of research for the Rhode Island Constitutional Convention.

Professor Cornwell is a graduate of Williams College and took his masters and doctoral degrees at Harvard University. He taught at Williams and at Princeton University before coming to the Brown University faculty in 1955.

OBVIOUSLY THE PRESS PLAYS an absolutely crucial role in presidential politics. It is equally true, but perhaps less obvious, that presidential politics are of great importance to the press. Furthermore, this reciprocal relationship is by no means limited to the American political and journalistic scene. National executives everywhere are becoming more plebiscitary. Their ties with their publics have become ever closer, and hence their dependence on the media ever greater.

These assertions border on being truisms. Before we can apply them to the American presidency and, for comparison, with the British prime ministership, a degree of semantic precision must be introduced. What, after all, does one mean by "politics" in this context? For immediate purposes the term "politics" may be defined as the process of persuasion, present in any political system, but most vigorously and obviously present in a democracy. The term is by no means limited to party politics or partisanship in this sense. Even electoral politics are only part of the story.

Obviously the word "press" at this point in history must be taken to encompass the electronic media as well as the printed page. However, since radio has been given over so widely to the dissemination of the teen culture, television necessarily carries the responsibility over the air. "Role" might be taken to suggest a passive relationship to presidential politics: that of a more or less neutral common carrier of information and opinion. Yet the press "role" in reality is seen to be far more active when examined closely. As seller of news, it seeks out material to purvey, focussing on certain types of "news" that have proven most readily saleable. Thus, the role of the press as envisioned here is activist in part and also self-serving in part.

In these terms, a more definitive title for this chapter might be: the interaction of the media of mass communication with the president in relation to the latter's efforts at persuasion and, thus, of governance. A few sentences from *Time* magazine of December 6, 1968, succinctly summarize the relations of the press to presidential politics:

> Every recent Administration—not only Johnson's but also Dwight Eisenhower's and John Kennedy's —has been accused of manipulating the news, or at least of an occasional lack of candor. The press wants to know everything, preferably before it happens and perferably handed to it on a silver platter. Presidents and their Administrations naturally want to feed out information as they see fit, preferably in such a way as to make them look good. p. 16

This is a familiar view of the president attempting to use the press for his ends, but also shows the less often explicit picture of press attempts to use the president for its own purposes. Presidents invariably seek to effectively persuade the press and to keep errors and less popular activities out of the public gaze. The press in quest of saleable news finds failures are more interesting than successes, corruption more exciting than dull virtue, backroom negotiations more fun than that which is in plain sight of all. Clearly the relation of press to White House is an antagonistic one. Their divergent goals produce frictions inasmuch as what one wants concealed the other wants to expose, and estimates of newsworthiness are bound to diverge often.

Yet for all this potential for conflict and competition, there are points of tangency and possibilities for cooperation in the relationship. Some stories find both sides bent on maximum play; often the president can help reporters by providing a useful lead on a dull day; or the press can help the executive by exercising discretion in the national interest.

The dynamics of the relationship are potentially more subtle and complex, however. Presidents—or Prime Ministers—if they are shrewd realize that they do not necessarily maximize their persuasion of the public through lectures and exhortations. They may well persuade more effectively by who they are, or appear to be, than by what they say. The citizenry's capacity for information and argumentation is less than its capacity to absorb and respond to images projected by public figures, political and otherwise. A political leader's successfully projected appearance of competence, concern, sincerity, his image in a word, can carry a far greater impact than his utterances. The skillful executive will, thus, do all that he can to create and project a favorable image for himself, to build up and conserve what might be termed his "image capital." He knows that wise investment of this capital will pay better dividends than mere exhortation.

Journalists, too, know that personalities are more interesting to readers than events (and events more interesting than speeches, one might add), and that leadership successes and failures are more interesting than the ebb and flow of policies. The press thus clearly recognizes, for its own part, the importance of public images, and has been known to create them when none is readily apparent. At times this creation is conscious; at other times the adroit public figure can induce the media to project his image by playing on its thirst for personalized and "human interest" news. Thus the interaction of the press and the executive can have a substantial impact on political outcomes, both personal and policy.

From the point of view of a political scientist it is more congenial to attempt to untangle some strands of this interwoven relationship from the governmental rather than from the journalistic point of view. Looking only at the recent presidential careers of John Kennedy and Lyndon Johnson, one cannot help being struck by the enormous importance of the factor of "image capital" in each and by the major role played by the mass media. My recent research in Britain revealed a similar situation among Prime Ministers, especially Harold Wilson and his predecessor once removed, Harold Macmillian. Each of these four national leaders dealt consciously and deliberately in the coinage of image capital. They have invested this capital in such a way as to reap substantial political dividends which probably could not have accrued in any other way. Yet each (with the obvious exception of Kennedy) has ended his stay in office with an empty image account if not, to push the analogy one step further, in bankruptcy. (This may be an unfair prejudgment of Harold Wilson, yet all the signs point toward his ultimate bankruptcy.)

Before attempting to draw some tentative conclusions it is necessary to examine the mechanics of this process of accumulation and use of image capital. These four political figures, as well as many others one could name, such as DeGaulle, the master manipulator of mass media, have known and respected the *potential* of the media in politics. (Certainly not all aspirants are blessed with this awareness.) They have accepted the legitimacy of this potential and its exploitation, unlike some of their more squeamish predecessors, and they have exercised considerable skill in contriving means for that exploitation. Also, they have actively accumulated and husbanded their supplies of image capital by cultivating the media and devising means of gaining access to them. Their object has been to project not just policies but favorable images of themselves as effective, trustworthy, and appealing political leaders.

John Kennedy clearly fits this pattern. He cultivated the working press, the columnists, and others who form the bridge between the public figure and the unseen constituency. He was perhaps more accessible to journalists seeking personal interviews than any president in history. His live televised press conferences generated unprecedented interest as he effectively capitalized on his skills as a communicator as well as on his physical and personality assets. His rocking chair interviews, so-called, were perhaps the most successful use of television yet devised for effective image and policy projection. Due largely to these efforts, Kennedy was able to turn his paper-thin 1960 margin of electoral victory into a vast fund of sympathy and support.

With some variations, Lyndon Johnson followed a similar program of media utilization. The circumstances of his accession to office solved at a stroke any problem he might have had in initial image capital accumulation. The nation was overwhelmingly his during that hour of trial. Nevertheless, he avidly husbanded and attempted to increase his capital hoard. His public relations activities were almost frenzied in the early months. He was constantly appearing on TV, whirling about the country, holding impromptu press conferences, and having journalists in for coffee. A striking contribution to the technology of image building was the installation in the White House of facilities to enable him to make spur-of-the-moment appearances on television. He was, thus, able to give the kind of triumphant announcements of which he was fond, and which he wanted to make *himself*. There was an element of overkill in all of this, a lack of subtlety and timing which sets his activity apart from Kennedy's more measured approach. There was also less sensitivity and his efforts to convey competence, sincerity, and fervent effort often were projected as deviousness, cloying folksiness, and egotism. Still, at the time of the 1964 election, his efforts seemed to have won for him a very widespread national support.

Turning to the other side of the Atlantic, one discerns strikingly similar patterns. True to the British national tendency to understate, underplay, and veil the harshness of their activities, No. 10 press and media relations have not been conducted or exposed to view with the same abandon as those of the White House. Furthermore, even following Lloyd George's quite unabashed use of the techniques of publicity, there was a gentlemanly reticence among British Prime Ministers when it came to the public relations arts. It was felt that there was something inappropriate if not downright indecent about crass self-advertisement. Thus, though the media and the theory for their use were available in Britain as early as in the United States, conscious exploitation lagged behind developments in Washington.

The more or less coincidental advent of television and of Harold Macmillan spelled the beginnings of a shift in both attitude and practice. A close examination of the career of Macmillan is therefore instructive. An Edwardian, if not a Victorian, he is naturally a shy man, steeped in all of the aristocratic traditions which would make publicity seeking distasteful. Accordingly, he did not seek a matey relationship with the working press and was, so it is said, distinctly uncomfortable in their company. Yet mateyness is less expected in Britain and although he did not himself cultivate the lobby correspondents (the rough equivalent of the White House correspondent group), his skillful public relations officer, Harold (later Sir Harold) Evans did gain their confidence and admiration. Though barely known to the P.M. when he took over his post in No. 10, Evans soon became a trusted associate of Macmillan, and thus was given considerable scope in doing his job.

The Prime Minister himself was not by any means wholly without publicity sense. He adopted such shrewd devices as making important speeches on Saturday so they would get full play in the thin Sunday and Monday papers. Also, he exploited the theatrical and publicity possibilities of trips abroad. Many will still recall his trip to Moscow which was made memorable by the huge fur hat which he affected, more for its eye-catching value, one can safely assume, than for its protection against the harsh Russian climate. On another occasion he had planned a Commonwealth tour. On the eve of his departure potentially damaging cabinet resignations occurred, which, when quizzed at the airport, the Prime Minister airily dismissed as minor difficulties. From incidents like this grew his reputation for monumental imperturbability. He also discovered that the airport interview, as a kind of substitute for a press conference, could be valuable and also, by virtue of its setting, quite attention-arresting.

Macmillan's major problem when he came to office in the wake of Anthony Eden's enforced departure was to rally his party from the disarray into which the Suez debacle had thrown it. Television proved the ultimate means to that end, although somewhat by accident. Early in his tenure of office, Macmillan was interviewed by Ed Murrow who, with characteristic skill, brought out all that was most attractive and reassuring in the new national leader. The interview made a tremendous impact in Britain, providing grist for the press for days afterward, a fact that was by no means lost on the P.M. Macmillan took full advantage of the opportunity thus revealed and made further appearances on interview shows. The image of "Super-Mac," tweedy yet shrewd, relaxed, and above all the unflappable national leader, gained wide and enthusiastic acceptance. Through it the British seemingly regained some of their shaken national self-confidence, in somewhat the fashion that F.D.R.'s confident image restored American morale in 1933. Thanks also to this leadership image the renaissance of the Tory party was rapid.

Harold Wilson came to the leadership of the Labour Party with an initial image capital balance at least as modest as Macmillan's had been. He was chosen for the post in the aftermath of the death of Hugh Gaitskell whose popularity had begun to catch hold, and whose untimely death was widely mourned. He had also to fight a bruising battle with George Brown for the leadership. Of the two, Brown was doubtless the more popular and widely known. In leadership terms, as well, Wilson's problem resembled Macmillan's. He had to inspire confidence in himself in order to convince the electorate that his party could govern responsibly. Labour has always suffered from a general public feeling that it is too addicted to obscure dogma, factionalism, and bitter infighting to be entrusted with national responsibility. The period between the fall of the Attlee government and Wilson's term of leadership was one in which these tendencies had been particularly and damagingly apparent.

After his selection as leader, Wilson spent two years in opposition, facing first the declining Macmillan and then, briefly, the "14th Earl" as Wilson derisively called Sir Alex Douglas-Home. During this period and after his narrow initial election victory, he worked systematically to create and build his image. Unlike his predecessor, he had a great fund of knowledge and skill in press relations. He knew and cultivated many lobby correspondents, knew the deadlines of the various papers, was aware of television production techniques, etc. It is said that as opposition leader he met regularly late Friday afternoons with three representatives of the Sunday papers, knowing that the stories he gave them could not be carefully checked before their press deadlines.

He also used, with striking success in the early years, the television interview that Macmillan had pioneered in British politics. His skill at the give and take of debate enabled him to take advantage of the interview format even though the questioning became increasingly sharp at the hands of interrogators like Robin Day. These prime ministerial appearances became quite frequent, and through the medium of television he was able to achieve an image of the skillful, trustworthy leader who promised to solve Britain's problems and to take the public uniquely into his confidence in the process.

His overall early performance and the flattery represented by his close personal relations with the working press so dazzled the latter that they could hardly write in sufficiently laudatory terms. The lobby correspondents, and especially the small group that was invited from time to time for an intimate chat with the Prime Minister, became his willing publicists.

Possibly taking a leaf from Macmillan's approach, though more likely arriving at the same conclusion independently, Wilson used trips abroad as generators of publicity and confirmers of his image. Two such forays to negotiate with Ian Smith, the prime minister of renegade Rhodesia, suggest his technique. Both involved the rather exotic surroundings of negotiation on shipboard at a point more or less midway between their two capitals. Both, significantly, took place on the same days that the Tory Annual Conference was meeting in Britain, hence enabling Wilson to steal the headlines for himself and relegate the frustrated Conservative leaders to the back pages. Harold Wilson, like the other Harold before him, was able to use the image capital thus acquired to solve temporarily (as it turned out) the problem of his party's right to rule. In 1966 he won a smashing electoral victory, turning his initial narrow margin of two years earlier into a very comfortable one. One need not, however, rely on this kind of indirect evidence of successful image building.

Polls, of course, provide another way of measuring accumulated image capital. Johnson, for example, began his tenure in office with an amazing 80 per cent favorable response to the Gallup question "Do you approve or disapprove of the way the President is handling his job?" LBJ remained above the 60 per cent favorable response level into the early months of 1966. When similar questions were asked in Britain, it was established that Wilson took office at No. 10 well above 50 per cent, climbed above 60 per cent in mid-1965 and reached the low 70 per cents in early 1966. Both Johnson and Wilson then went into a sharp decline which caused them to hit lows in the 30 per cent range during 1968. Vietnam precipitated the run on Johnson's capital, as devaluation, and its maladroit portrayal to the nation, did for Wilson's.

In a phrase that was to come back to haunt him time and time again, hurled gleefully from across the aisle in the House of Commons, Wilson insisted rather disingenuously in his televised explanation of devaluation that "the pound in your pocket has not been devaluated." This was true in one sense, but in terms of the price rises that followed the cut in the pound for the consumer, it was hardly true in fact. The statement came to symbolize the credibility gap that was opening up between Wilson and the press (and public) just as it did in the United States for Lyndon Johnson. Reporters, misled by the Prime Minister's lack of candor, increasingly distrusted him, and adulatory writing turned to skepticism and hostility. Both leaders enjoyed the initial advantages of carefully developed and husbanded image capital. Both, however, tended to overplay their image building, becoming in the eyes of the press, and through the press of the public, "too clever by half," as the British would put it. Both, too, encountered devastatingly difficult policy problems from which no amount of image capital could have purchased release or immunity.

The conclusion to be drawn is not that political leaders who worry about the construction and manipulation of their images come to no good end. The Johnson and Wilson experiences require a more subtle interpretation. Disraeli, in one of my favorite gleanings from him, once said, "with words we govern men." Today we might rephrase that "with public relations we govern men." If a national political leader chooses not to use the arts of public relations and the opportunities inherent in the media to build and use the assets of image capital, he runs even greater risks than the leader who does. By such a self-denying ordinance he deprives himself of one of the most potent means of exercising influence and wielding power open to contemporary statesmen. Ideally, perhaps, electorates should respond most readily to reasoned arguments and careful explanations of policy proposals. In fact, however, they respond to images which inspire trust and confidence and accept programs because of their sponsorship rather than because of their perceived intrinsic merit.

It is, of course, true that image manipulation is a dangerous game. Even when used with skill and subtlety, image capital is a wasting asset. Able indeed is the leader who spends his in such a way as to achieve his goals without a deficit at the end of his term. Image capital must be spent (invested) to bring returns in policy accomplishments. When a leader lays capital on the line to purchase support, he inevitably loses some of it by alienating those who oppose the policy or recoil from his partisan involvement. Leaders, like Eisenhower, who refuse to spend their capital will leave office with a credit balance but few accomplishments.

It will, of course, be very interesting to see how current and future national leaders resolve the problem. There is already evidence that Richard

Nixon has drawn the conclusion that image building is too dangerous to attempt. Past dealings with the press hold unpleasant memories for him and certainly the Johnson "credibility gap" is to be avoided. We are seeing the carefully staged press appearances combined with the two-platoon, in-depth staff arrangement with Ronald Ziegler as press secretary backed by Herbert Klein as director of communications. Yet Gallup found only an initial 61 per cent approval rate for Nixon compared with 79 per cent for Johnson, 72 per cent for Kennedy and 68 per cent for Ike at similar points in their presidency. The question remains whether Nixon can afford not to try and build his capital account.

Ted Heath, the Tory heir apparent to Wilson, seems also to have decided to avoid the risks of image projection. Heath, like Nixon, if he comes to office, will do so with few image assets. Yet the nations that these men seek to lead face problems of excruciating difficulty and enormous complexity. In both cases, although the solutions will not be contrived easily, the major problem will be securing public acceptance for them. To attain this acceptance, image capital in the form of trust and confidence will be indispensable.

It goes without saying that all of this is crucial

to an understanding of "The Role of the Press in Presidential (or Prime Ministerial) Politics" even though I have trod only lightly on the role of the press itself. If there are moral questions involved, they are not necessarily questions of who is exploiting whom. The very nature of the functioning of democratic political systems today is involved in these relationships.

CHAPTER TWO

Appraising Press Coverage of Politics

by

William L. Rivers

Professor of Communication
Stanford University

WILLIAM L. RIVERS, professor of communication at Stanford University, has written extensively on the relationship of the press and politics. His book, *The Opinionmakers*, an examination of the Washington press corps, won the Sigma Delta Chi Distinguished Research Award in 1966.

Professor Rivers was a Congressional Fellow in the 1950's, working as an assistant to Senator J. William Fulbright. In the early 1960's he was a Washington correspondent for *The Reporter*. He was awarded a doctorate in political science at American University and served as a faculty member at the universities of Texas, Louisiana State, and Miami before going to Stanford.

In addition to *The Opinionmakers*, Professor Rivers is author of *The Mass Media, The Adversaries: Politics and the Press*, and co-authored *Responsibility in Mass Communication* with Wilbur Schramm, and *The Mass Media and Modern Society* with Theodore Peterson and Jay Jensen. His articles on press and politics have appeared in *Saturday Review, Harpers, Nation, New York Times Magazine*, and *Columbia Journalism Review*. International studies in press and politics were carried out by Professor Rivers through fellowships awarded to him by the North Atlantic Treaty Organization.

I CAN BEGIN BY SAYING quite confidently that the reporting of politics and governmental affairs is better today than it has ever been. But that's hardly very descriptive. After all, accomplishment that is better than it has ever been may not be good enough. And that, I think, is an appropriate keynote for my comments: Reporting today is fast, accurate, thoughtful, and not nearly good enough.

Thus, I find myself complimenting political journalists today much in the manner of the acid adolescent who was instructed by his mother that he was to compliment his date when the dance was over. And so it was that the boy said to his date at the end of the evening, "You sweat less than any fat girl I ever danced with."

It is not helpful, though, to deal in compliments, left-handed or otherwise, and it is even less helpful to attack without understanding. And so our chief task is to try to understand why political journalism fails, to grapple with the reasons for failure. We can deal with all of them, I think, under a single heading: Inhibitions of the Truth. Why is the truth about political affairs inhibited? For these reasons:

First, because journalists, like their readers, listeners, and viewers, are subject to the selective processes.

We expose our senses primarily to information that reinforces our own ideas. This the psychologists call *selective exposure*. In one test of it, Wilbur Schramm and Richard Carter of Stanford University found that Republicans are almost twice as likely as Democrats to watch a Republican-sponsored telecast. We also tend to see what we want to see—*selective perception*—which social researchers have shown so often that they now have approximately the same compulsion to demonstrate it again that a mathematician has to show that two plus two equals four. Some of us go to ludicrous lengths to perceive "facts" that will support our prejudices. In one experiment, anti-Semites looked at editorial cartoons that ridiculed religious bias and saw them in reverse—as glorifications of Anglo-Saxon lineage. And we unconsciously remember facts that enhance our own views—*selective retention*. Shortly after Lyndon Johnson was elected president, groups of pro-Johnson college students and groups of anti-Johnson students were asked to study a highly laudatory article about him. The pro-Johnson students learned the pro-Johnson facts sooner and remembered them longer.

Now a journalist is less likely than the layman to be misled by selective exposure. After all, if a Democratic reporter is assigned to cover the speech of a Republican candidate, he covers it. But journalists are as subject to the other processes as anyone, and I think an example from my own experience—an example that illustrated my most grievous mistake as a reporter—shows the point.

This occurred when I was working as a Washington correspondent for *The Reporter* magazine in 1960 when John F. Kennedy and Richard M. Nixon were candidates for the presidency. One night shortly before the election, I covered a curious political-religious convocation of the African Methodist Episcopal Church during which Senator Hugh Scott of Pennsylvania claimed that Richard Nixon had, in effect, integrated a Missouri motel. The story Senator Scott told had Nixon refusing to let his campaign entourage put up at the motel unless a Negro member of the group was allowed to stay there with the others. Now I didn't like Mr. Nixon, and I didn't think he would do anything so forthright. In short, I didn't believe Scott. After taking detailed notes on the many other aspects of the convocation, I returned to my office that night and telephoned the motel. Was it true, I asked the manager, that Nixon had refused to allow his campaign entourage to put up at the motel if the segregation policy was not changed immediately? "Yes, that's true," the manager said, "and we're still integrated."

The next morning, I wrote this report on the convocation. All the facts I cite are true, but the omission is significant:

The Republican campaign to convince Negro voters that Senator John Kennedy has two positions on civil rights—one for Northern audiences and another for listeners in the South—took some questionable turns recently at the national "Convocation of Faith" of the million-member African Methodist Episcopal Church. Announcing that the convocation was also "a platform for Christian statesmanship," Bishop James Madison Reid said that he had been rewarded when he asked the Republican National Committee to send over some "big timber" for the closing session. "This," he said, gesturing proudly toward Jackie Robinson and Senator Hugh Scott (R., Pennsylvania), "looks like big timber to me."

Bishop Reid had not asked the Democrats to supply corresponding timber. In fact, the Bishop himself — who credits former Ambassador Henry Cabot Lodge with bringing fourteen African nations into the United Nations and "sending Ralph Bunche to Africa"—delivered two strong speeches for the Republican ticket, then punctuated the other addresses with "Yes!" and "Amen!"

Robinson, whose standing was attested by the appreciative nods and murmurs that greeted his allusions to "Rickey" and "the Dodgers" and "Chock Full O'Nuts," was appealingly direct in explaining why he supports Vice President Nixon.

He had been for Senator Hubert Humphrey, but when Humphrey failed to get the Democratic nomination, Robinson braced both of the nominees on civil rights. "Nixon looked me straight in the eye when he answered my questions. . . .Senator Kennedy looked at Chester Bowles."

Robinson also alluded to the fact that "Vice President Nixon went into Jackson, Mississippi, and spoke for civil rights." But it was left to Senator Scott to build most of the case against Kennedy. Announcing that he was going to "call the roll on Senator Kennedy's lack of courage"—and getting repeated urgings from Bishop Reid to "Call the roll!"—Scott devoted most of his speech to it. For nearly an hour Scott found new ways to say that "This Harvard college boy . . . this rich Ivy Leaguer who has lived high on the hog all his life . . . is vocal in the North and silent in the South. Senator Kennedy has never yet mentioned civil rights in the South."

Senator Scott probably reached a new low in church oratory when he said that "Kennedy has never even integrated a bathroom," but it is unlikely that anyone will want to debate that point with him. It is a matter of record, however, that Senator Kennedy has spoken out on civil rights in the South. In Greenville, North Carolina, he said, ". . . every American regardless of his race or religion is entitled to his constitutional rights." In Memphis: "I want to see an America which is free *for everyone, which protects the constitutional rights of every American, which will serve as our own symbol, our own identification with the cause of freedom."*

Perhaps most important, Senator Kennedy said in Jackson, Mississippi, in October, 1957: "I have no hesitancy in saying the same thing that I have said in my own city of Boston: that I have accepted the Supreme Court decision as the supreme law of the land." This had apparently escaped Senator Scott's convenient memory, for he told the Negro churchmen, "Senator Kennedy has very suddenly, since he became a candidate, developed an interest in your problems."

It was left to Republican Chairman Thruston Morton to supply the irony: On the day Scott rewrote the record, Morton made him a member of the Republican "Truth Squad."

The fact is, of course, that *my* memory was more convenient than Scott's. Nowhere did I point out that Richard Nixon integrated a motel, a fact which certainly would have helped win Negro votes to his cause. I did not omit this consciously. My prejudices did the work and I was unaware of it until, much later, I read about the phenomenon known as "selective perception."

The way to guard against such inhibitions of the truth, I think, is to make ourselves acutely sensitive to the danger. We are human, and we will make human errors, but the journalist who studies and analyzes the selective processes reduces his subjugation to them.

I must make it clear, before leaving this area of deep concern, how unpredictable the audiences of the news media actually are. They are predictable up to a point. By that I mean that they, too, will continue to be subject to the selective processes that influence us all. They will indulge themselves in selective exposure; they will continue to expose their minds largely to that with which they already agree. They will be guilty of selective perception; that is, they will see what they want to see. They will guard their prejudices with selective retention. Thus, they will retain precisely what they want to retain so as to remain in uninjured possession of their quirks and idiosyncrasies.

But then, to confound everyone who hopes to predict human behavior, the audiences of the mass media will occasionally demonstrate their essential independence. I know of no better example than the letters that reached *Time* magazine shortly after the publication of a long article on Dr. Fred Schwarz, the Australian who runs the Christian Anti-Communism Crusade. It seemed to me that the article had been suitably even-handed in dealing out pros and cons on Schwarz. That is, *Time* played the story straight down the middle—for a change. The interesting aspect, though, is not the article, but the reader response to it.

The first letter ran:

Sir:

Just finished reading your article on "Crusader Schwarz," and my only reaction is this: What is he doing in our country? He should be expelled as an undesirable alien!

Palmer B. Rowley, Jr.

The next correspondent saw a different side:

Sir:

What America needs are more crusaders like Dr. Schwarz. He and others like him, who are free from the subversive secrecy of organizations like the John Birch Society, will surely be most instrumental in the final victory over world communism.

Charles A. Piddock

The third correspondent, obviously a Schwarz supporter, was certain *Time* was castigating Schwarz:

Sir:

I am truly dismayed at the nasty way you degraded Dr. Schwarz in your article.

Eva V. Burnham

That response makes the fourth letter the most interesting of all:

Sir:

Congratulations for your very fine report on the Christian Anti-Communism Crusade. This is an example of thorough and unbiased reporting that is truly admirable.

Fred Schwarz
President

If the inhibitions of truth that these examples illustrate are fairly well known to students of the ghostly science called psychology, the second inhibition is much less widely known.

I speak now of the concept of journalistic elites. It is, at least potentially, the most damaging of all. Now the concept of elites in general is also widely known. I can illustrate it by saying that if all of you in this audience were to stay together in a continuing seminar for a week or so, studying some issue of moment, a deft psychologist could at the end of that time point quite positively to the elite among you— to those who lead the opinions of the others. Unfortunately, the concept of a journalistic elite has not been studied sufficiently, but I think I can make it clear *as an affliction* by citing a paragraph from an article by Meg Greenfield, and another paragraph from a book by Victor Lasky. Miss Greenfield wrote an article on Richard Nixon in 1960— and the year is important to my story. One paragraph of her article ran:

The standard pattern of Nixon's prose goes something like this: statement of one side of the case (A), followed by a statement of the other side of the case (B). Although the bridge from (A) to (B) is usually the word "but," other familiar locutions such as "at the same time," "on the other hand," and "however" also enable him to take a position and warn against it at the same time.

Three years later, Victor Lasky published his attack on Kennedy titled *J.F.K. The Man And The Myth.* We find on page 358:

The standard pattern of Kennedy's prose went something like this: statement of one side of the case (A), followed by a statement of the other side of the case (B). Although the bridge from (A) to (B) is usually the word "but," other familiar locutions such as "at the same time," "on the other hand," and "however" also enabled him to take a position and warn against it at the same time.

This is much more than an item that should rank high in any responsible survey of plagiarism. It is a small indication of how restricted the journalistic investigative process really is. We have more than a thousand Washington correspondents. But do we have a thousand probes into government? The answer is clearly negative. We have hundreds pursuing a single story—and duplicating each other. We have the herd instinct that has Meg Greenfield turning a phrase, and someone taking it.

We have the herd instinct that has Walter Lippmann developing an insight—and then days and weeks after he publishes it, many other journalists developing the same insight. We have the herd instinct that has James Reston setting forth the meaning of a government policy—to be followed by many others who explore the same meaning of the same policy.

So instead of a thousand individual probes into government, we have a score, or perhaps two-score—made up of clusters of correspondents who lean heavily on their elites.

It is not quite true that one can learn everything worth learning about political journalism by reading the *New York Times*, *The Washington Post*, *The Washington Evening Star*, the *Los Angeles Times*, and the *Baltimore Sun*, and perhaps listening to Eric Sevareid, but that is close enough to the truth to call into serious question the herd instinct that afflicts journalism.

But the most important inhibition of truth in political reporting can be charged to government. And it always could be. Nothing is more absurd than thinking of news control by government as a modern phenomenon. The focus on credibility may be sharper today, but the truth is that information policy has been at the very center of governing the United States from the beginning.

Patrick Henry set the terms of the historic debate. The government, he said, must keep from the press "such transactions as relate to military operations or affairs of great consequence, the immediate promulgation of which might defeat the interests of the community." The press must prevent officials from "covering with the veil of secrecy the common routine of business, for the liberties of the people never were, or never will be, secure when the transactions of their rulers may be concealed from them."

The great question has always been: which are the affairs which might "defeat the interests of the community?" The writing of the Constitution was deemed to be one. The delegates of the Constitutional Convention straggled into Philadelphia in May of 1787—their deliberations began nearly two weeks late—but for all the apathetic atmosphere they were agreed from the beginning that drafting a new form of government, or shoring up the old one, would be impossible if their speeches were published piecemeal and debated on every village square. They took a pledge of secrecy.

There seemed to be good reason for a secret convention. Had the masses of Americans been able to read of some of the more extreme proposals, the convention hall might have been a focus for rioting. Brilliant, ambitious, thoroughly aristocratic Alexander Hamilton, holding that the "rich and well-born" must be given their "distinct, permanent share in the government;" smooth Cotesworth Pinckney politely threatening the withdrawal of South Carolina if the majority carried through its plan to abolish the slave trade; endless compromising on the part of several delegates whose public posture was inflexible principle—all this went on behind bolted doors.

One day a delegate carelessly mislaid his copy of the proposals. It was found and turned over to George Washington, the president of the Convention. He seemed to ignore it, but as the meeting was adjourning for the day, Washington stated grimly: "Gentlemen, I am sorry to find that some one member of this body has been so neglectful of the secrets of the Convention as to drop in the State House a copy of their proceedings, which by accident was picked up and delivered to me this morning. I must entreat gentlemen to be more careful, lest our transactions get into the news papers and disturb the public response by premature speculations."

Until James Madison's notes were published decades later, few Americans had any real knowledge of what had occurred during the Constitutional Convention.

Other powerful leaders were as convinced as

was Patrick Henry that the common routine of government business must be publicized. They believed that the survival of the new nation depended upon information that would in Thomas Jefferson's phrase, "penetrate the whole mass of the people." Madison, the father of the Constitution, wrote: "Knowledge will forever govern ignorance. And a people who mean to be their own governors must arm themselves with the power knowledge gives. A popular government without popular information or the means of acquiring it, is but a prologue to a farce, or a tragedy, or perhaps both."

Clearly, the founders considered informing the people to be a function of democracy. But they carefully refrained from setting up an official information system. Instead, the informing function was turned over to the press. In effect, the press—privately owned, beyond official control—was incorporated into the machinery of democratic government.

Surely, some of the genius of the American idea flows from the fact that the apparatus of information was made an independent part of the continuing government in a way that insured its freedom from any particular administration. Officials from the first have had to adapt to the anomaly of an information system that is *of*, but not *in*, the government. This established a natural struggle between the men of the press and the men of the official government. It is no accident that the "strong presidents" revered by many historians and political scientists—Washington, Jefferson, Jackson, Lincoln, Theodore Roosevelt, and Franklin Roosevelt—are also the presidents who have most adroitly manipulated information. Much of the history of American government pivots on the use of the press as an instrument of political power.

We can get a clear idea of just how important publicity has been to every government leader, I think, if we focus on the comment George Washington made to Alexander Hamilton as they were considering a draft of the Farewell Address. Washington, the man we think of as austere, above the battle, said: "The doubt that occurs at first view is the length of it for a newspaper publication. All the columns of a large gazette would scarcely, I conceive, contain the present draft."

It is not very far from that preoccupation with publicity to Andrew Jackson's whole-souled attempt to control what was said about *his* administration by putting 57 journalists on the government payroll. Jackson, one noted historian has written, "was the first president who ruled the country by means of the newspaper press."

He was not the last. The great Lincoln may

have been as adroit as anyone at using the press. It was Lincoln who said: "In this and like communities, public sentiment is everything. With public sentiment, nothing can fail. Without it, nothing can succeed. Consequently, he who moulds public sentiment goes deeper than he who enacts statutes and pronounces decisions." Lincoln proved his adeptness by refusing to release the Emancipation Proclamation spontaneously when it was written. Instead, like a far-seeing public relations man, he picked the propitious moment. He waited two months. Then the advantage seemed to be on the Union side at the battle of Antietam, and he released the Proclamation.

That has been the pattern throughout our history. Public officials, believing in their plans and programs, have always sought to shape the news, to manage it, to twist it to their advantage. It is difficult to think of them harshly if we grant that they truly *believe* that their programs are in the public interest.

And so it is that we reached the culmination of government control of the news during the Johnson administration. Mr. Johnson was the beneficiary of all the experiences, not to mention the ploys and gambits, of all the other officials who preceded him. It is not surprising that he used all their techniques. And, given the temper of the man, it is even less surprising that he went too far, tipped the scales too definitely his way—and fell resoundingly. As one of the correspondents said of him: "Any politician who is so clever as to meet himself coming around the corner always finds someone waiting there to remind him where he has been."

An example will indicate one of Mr. Johnson's techniques:

While Johnson was Senate Majority Leader, Stewart Alsop wrote an article suggesting that Democrats as well as Republicans were vulnerable on the defense issue. The article contained these two fatal sentences: "As for Johnson, his voting record on defense has been good. But he is obviously open to the charge that he only summoned his preparedness subcommittee to make a serious inquiry into preparedness after the issue had been dramatized by the Sputniks."

Alsop later wrote:

> . . . on the day the article appeared, the reporter was summoned to the majority leader's small, ornate, oddly impressive office in the capitol. Treatment A started quietly. The majority leader was, it seemed, in a relaxed, friendly, and reminiscent mood. Nostalgically he recalled how he had come to Washington in 1937, a mere freshman congressman, and how Franklin D.

Roosevelt had prevailed on the chairman of the Naval Affairs Committee to put "Young Lyndon Johnson" on his powerful committee. That was, it seemed, the beginning of Johnson's interest in the national defense, which had continued ever since.

By gradual stages the relaxed, friendly and reminiscent mood gave way to something rather like a human hurricane. Johnson was up, striding about his office, talking without pause, occasionally leaning over, his nose almost touching the mesmerized reporter's, to shake the reporter's shoulder or grab his knee. Secretaries were rung for. Memoranda appeared and then more memoranda, as well as letters, newspaper articles and unidentifiable scraps of paper, which were proffered in quick succession and then snatched away. Appeals were made, to the Almighty, to the shades of the departed great, to the reporter's finer instincts and better nature, while the reporter, unable to get a word in edgewise, sat collapsed upon a leather sofa, eyes glazed, mouth half open. Treatment A ended a full two hours later, when the majority leader, a friendly arm around the shoulder of the dazed journalist, ushered him into the outer office. It was not until some days later that the reporter was able to recall that, excellent as Johnson's record on national defense undoubtedly is, the two sentences he had written had been demonstrably true.

That, of course, is what is meant by "Come, let us reason together."

Mr. Johnson's sensitivity to publicity is suggested by his installing AP and UPI teletype machines in his office. Wire service editors could expect complaints from Mr. Johnson before the reports were published or broadcast.

It is far too early to tell what Mr. Nixon's experiences will be, or what techniques he will use as president. The only certainty is that his relations with the press corps will, sooner or later, become abrasive. How wide or deep the Nixon credibility gap will be is unknown. But there will be one. There always *has* been one. Officials and journalists have such differing responsibilities that an adversary relationship is essential at some point.

All these inhibitions of the truth—the selective processes that afflict journalists and their audiences, the elites that limit the journalistic corps' work, and the continuing adversary relationship with government—all these inhibitions assure that political journalism cannot be ultimately pure, ultimately truthful. And yet it is clear to anyone who has studied political journalism that Walter Lippmann is right when he looks back across half a century of journalism. He once called political journalism "a refuge for the vaguely talented." Now, he says, "It has improved immensely. The political reporters today *think*."

CHAPTER THREE

Politicians and Biased Political Information

by

David S. Broder

Political Columnist
The Washington Post

DAVID S. BRODER has the reputation of a reporter who does his homework. In 1968, *Newsweek* referred to Mr. Broder as the political reporter's political reporter. *Time*, the same week, said that the Washington press corps views Mr. Broder as perhaps the nation's top political correspondent.

Mr. Broder holds undergraduate and graduate degrees from the University of Chicago. After graduation and a period with the Army, he became a member of the staff of the Bloomington (Ill.) *Daily Pantagraph*. In the mid-1950's Mr. Broder moved to Washington to become political correspondent for the *Congressional Quarterly*, where, according to *Time*, he developed his passion for detail. He moved from the *Quarterly* to *The Washington Evening Star* as a political reporter and correspondent, then, after five years with the *Star*, became a Washington political observer for the *New York Times*. He resigned from the *Times* to become a political analyst and columnist for *The Washington Post*.

Mr. Broder is co-author, with Stephen Hess, of *The Republican Establishment*, and he is a frequent contributor to *Atlantic*, *Harpers*, *New York Times Magazine*, *Look*, and *New Republic*.

THE RELATIONSHIP BETWEEN the press and politics is a topic increasingly of concern to those of us who are working in newspapers, and I gather from the contacts I have had with politicians, also increasingly of concern to them. We have become in recent years—at least it seems to me in Washington—so involved in the antagonisms between the press and politics that we have forgotten what the common concerns are that we share in these two institutions—in the political institutions and the institutions of the press. We have even forgotten some of the common problems we share, not the least of which is that both of us—both politicians on their side and the press on the side that I'm involved with—have a very serious credibility gap problem. It never occurs to us that this is a common concern. I do think that there are common problems and common concerns that we have which we have not focused in on, and which I hope this kind of a series will bring to our attention and bring to your attention.

I want to stipulate at the very beginning that I am personally much more concerned about the failings and the distortions of the press than I am about the bias of politicians. But I am going to direct my remarks to the subject I was asked to talk about, which is the way in which politicians influence the flow of news and information. I do want you to keep in mind that I do not wish to suggest or imply that the problems—the very real problems that exist in this area—are solely or even in a major degree the responsibility of the politicians. We in the press have much to answer for and much room for improvement in our part of that process.

Let me begin then, by talking about what I would consider two myths that cloud understanding of this issue of credibility, of public understanding of what the government is doing, of the flow of political information.

One is the myth—a journalistic myth, really—that argues that something we can honestly call objective news coverage can be obtained through a sort of universality of reporting. I used to work for the *New York Times*, which every day on its front page carries that wonderful slogan, "All the news that's fit to print." It's a splendid slogan, but it is a total fraud. If you think about it for a moment you'll know that it's a fraud, because even the *New York Times*, with the amount of space and the amount of staff resources that it can devote to covering the day's news, cannot begin to report all of the words and all of the events of significance to someone that occur on any given day in the city of Washington, let alone all the other cities where there are *Times* men at work gathering the news. Selectivity is the essence of all contemporary journalism, whether you are talking about the process at the *New York Times*, at *The Washington Post*, the *Baltimore Sun*, or at any of the other newspapers. A similar process under even more exacting limitations is involved in putting together the Huntley-Brinkley show or the Cronkite show each night. The problem that all of us live with constantly in journalism is what to leave out—what can safely be left out with minimum distorting effects. Of the millions of words, of the thousands of incidents, that occur on the political beat every day, which are going to be singled out for public attention?

Now, selectivity, which is the essence of the procedure, involves criteria. Criteria mean value judgments. And value judgments are just fancy words for prejudices. It seems to me that the beginning of wisdom about the journalistic side of the process is to recognize that there is no escape from this kind of procedure. We must learn to be aware of our prejudices and the built-in biases that we bring to this selection process. A standard of fairness—an open-eyed willingness to examine our own biases along with everybody else's—is possible, but we have to realize that there is no such thing as a totally neutral, objective portrait of the world that can emerge from contemporary journalism. By that I mean that if an event took place here in this room, none of us could agree on our description of exactly what had happened—that kind of objectivity is simply not attainable in the real world, at least from my point of view it is not.

The second myth, it seems to me, is a parallel one that goes directly to the topic we are concerned with today. It is the myth that there can somehow be a neutral relationship between a politician or public official and the reporter or the press. That relationship can be good or bad, it can be tense or relaxed, it can be smooth and workable or angry and contentious. It can be all of those different things, but whatever it is, it can never be a neutral relationship. And the reason I would suggest to you why it cannot is that the process of news dissemination, as the politician would view it, is inextricably involved with the whole process and the competition for power that is at the very essence of the governing process.

If you look at it from the politician's point of view, one channel to power for him is publicity—the ability to command attention for himself, for his projects, for his goals, and for his activities, as against all the others in public office or seeking public office who are also striving for attention.

That being the case, he looks on me as a reporter—
or on any reporter—as the one channel through
whom he hopes to get his story across that day;
through whom he hopes to be able to direct attention to himself and his activities, and, if possible, to
shape the understanding of those activities according to the interpretation that he would like to place
upon them.

Conversely, I come at this relationship as a reporter from a very different perspective. The com-
modity in which I deal as a reporter—the kind of
thing that represents power to me—is information,
and not just random information, but relevant information about events of some significance in the
area in which I'm working. The old saying—and it
sums it all up—is that a reporter is no better than
his sources. What is important to me is being able to
have access to men who are knowledgeable about a
situation at a time when that situation is in the public eye. So, I'm interested in them for what they can
give me—information about a subject that I'm pursuing. They're interested in me for what I can give
to them—a channel to the public for the goals in
which they are interested.

There is a kind of built-in tension in the relationship. It is, if you will, essentially a manipulative
relationship on both sides in which each party is at-

tempting to use the other for his own purposes. Now, we get into difficulty on both sides of this relationship when we fail to recognize it for what it is.

When the President of the United States says, for example, as Lyndon Johnson said to a group of reporters on Air Force One coming back to Washington shortly after he had become President, "You fellows play ball with me, and I'll make you big men," he seriously misunderstands the relationship of a politician, even if he is a President of the United States, to the reporters who are covering him. But equally, we on our side are naive or mistaken when we complain, as we do frequently, about politicians managing the news, because there's no way in the real world that I've observed in which we could ever expect politicians to leave the news unmanaged, not to shape it to their purposes.

Now, how do politicians bias the news, to come back directly to our topic. Well, there are many variations, but the common thread to the techniques that are used is what I would call the process of selective disclosure. As an example, from President Johnson—I take him not because I wish to suggest that he is the only one, but because, you know, we've had recent experience with him—I recall his campaign speech in Buffalo in the fall of 1966, one of the few polititical appearances he made there. In the course of this speech to a very large crowd in Buffalo he announced that the government was ready to experiment with a new process of sewage treatment and that they had chosen Lake Erie, right in Buffalo's backyard, as the first place they were going to conduct this experiment. He said he was very happy and proud to be able to announce "here in Buffalo in the presence of your wonderful young Democratic Congressman, Richard McCarthy, that we are going to have the first pilot program on this new kind of sewage treatment program right here in Lake Erie." What he did not tell them was that the plant was going to be built in Cleveland. That is an example of selective disclosure. He didn't tell them anything false, but he didn't tell them all that was relevant. When the Buffalo newspapers found out 24 hours later that the plant that they had all understood was coming to Buffalo was going to Cleveland instead, there was a little bit of an understandable reaction.

The same kind of process goes on, I suppose, in federal budget-making. Federal budgets are projected on the basis of the most optimistic set of assumptions possible—that user fees of certain kinds which Congress has each year rejected will this year be enacted; that popular programs like school lunch programs will be reduced; that the federal crop estimates will be at the low level rather than the high level. None of this is false, but when the assumptions that go into the budget are examined, the whole structure becomes much more dubious than the terms in which it is actually set forth to the country by the Administration.

It is again typical procedure in announcing new programs. The programs are announced, their long-term goals are described, but only in the small print is it indicated that the actual financing that has been requested for these programs in the first year or two is minimal.

We could multiply this example ad infinitum. This is what I would call a process of selective disclosure. The government official or the politician involved puts the emphasis deliberately on the aspect of what he is disclosing that is most favorable from the point of view of the objective that he has in mind. There are many variants of the thing. There is the variant where the politician elects to make no disclosure at all. For example, when the anti-ballistic missile program was going through Congress it was explained as a program to defend cities, but nowhere was it explained to the Congress, or at least the congressmen didn't understand, that the sites for these ABM installations were going to have to be right in the suburbs of the cities they were designed to defend. Once that fact was discovered, the political reaction to the ABM became quite different.

There is another technique which is familiar to all of us. It is the sort of press agentry of an event, something that may or may not be a real event but is handled in such a way that it commands attention. For example, the president might introduce his cabinet on national television. Or if he is having difficulty selling a war policy in Vietnam, he brings back the commanding general to address a joint session of Congress. Attention is commanded through this kind of artificial and dramatic device to display the side of the story that is sought.

I have tended to talk, I suppose, rather critically of these devices by which the politicians can bias, shape, or manage the news. I don't mean to suggest that these are necessarily evil. They are only evil if you think that politics as a process is evil, which I certainly do not.

Disclosure on a selective basis can have very useful political functions. For example, a disclosure or leak of information may be designed to prevent some action or policy which the person leaking the information thinks is inimical. For example, in my own reporting from within the Nixon Administration, I was told that Senator Strom Thurmond had been intervening at the Pentagon and the White House on a major case involving alleged segregation or the refusal to desegregate facilities of a major defense contractor. The reason the information was leaked to me was clearly that the person leaking it wanted to have some public attention directed to this as a way of negating what might be this particular senator's private bargaining power in the situation.

There is also the kind of disclosure that is planned to spur action. Another example from my own reporting was a tip a few years ago that the Department of Health, Education, and Welfare had done a very careful study of the extent of federal research on population and birth control. That report was being bottled up by political officials at the top of the department. In order to force those officials to disclose it, a portion of the report was deliberately leaked to a reporter—in this case, me.

An example of another kind of disclosure that happens very frequently is simply the testing of what the reaction would be if an event did occur. For example, while not really governmental, within the Democratic party: after key party leaders had given pretty good clearance on the choice of Senator George McGovern to head the Democratic Party Reform Committee, the fact that he was being seriously considered for that job was leaked. Why? Because if it appeared in a major newspaper in this way, they would have a chance to test the reaction of a large section of the Democratic party leadership without having to call these people individually. Anybody who saw that story in the paper and was going to go up in flames about the choice would have a chance to make his case, and the leaders would have a chance to test that reaction before they were formally committed to the choice of McGovern.

All of these methods are legitimate kinds and parts of the political process. But they all have in common an element of manipulation by the politicians or the public officials concerned, where the news media are used to achieve some specific purpose of the politicians in question. And knowing that this is a common pattern of political behavior breeds in the reporters—myself included—a rather skeptical attitude towards what politicians say.

It is at this point that you get the familiar argument of the politician saying to the reporter, "You guys are always trying to shoot holes in whatever we say." Former Secretary of State Dean Rusk is a rather exalted example of this; he said to reporters at the State Department, "Which side are you men on in this war?"

Here the kind of skepticism that becomes the reporter's defense against being manipulated and used by the politician becomes a major source of aggravation to the politician. And here is the beginning of the kind of exacerbation of personal and professional relationships which has characterized so much of the tenor of press and political, press and government relationships in Washington in recent years.

How do you deal with this kind of conflict as a journalist or in terms of a public policy—if there is a public policy problem involved? I'm inclined to think there is, because the skepticism about government and the skepticism about the press has now reached a degree in this country where I think it has become—if you view a free press and a representative government as worthwhile institutions to protect—a source of concern. How do you mediate the conflict? Are ground rules possible? If they are going to be found, they can only be found if we shift our perspective from a two-sided conflict or engagement or relationship between press and government, between politician and reporter, and look at both of them in terms of the essential third party to this transaction, which is the public. No government official in a country that operates on the theory that ours does, has a right to rule by fiat, in secrecy and in private. Similarly, no newspaper reporter as an individual has any personal right—it seems to me—to simply make himself a public nuisance on the thing. If either of them has to be judged, he has to be judged in terms of how well his behavior conforms to and assists the model that exists in our country, which is a representative government resting on—in some meaningful sense and not just a fictitious sense—the consent and the understanding of the governed. Standing on opposite sides of the room and hollering at each other, which is frequently the pattern of behavior in which press and politicians have found themselves, is really a futile kind of exercise. Both have an obligation which they have to remember. They must inform the public, so as to arm the public with the essential information that makes public policy decision a meaningful process. And that is an obligation which neither the politician nor the reporter can fulfill alone.

If you were to generalize—probably outrageously—and say you know what really is at the root of so much of the discontent with political institutions in this country, I think you would suppose it is the feeling that seems to be so widespread, and it goes from the ghetto to the affluent suburb, that events are taking place and decisions are being made in this political process without the meaningful understanding and participation of the people who are affected by those decisions. This is really an indictment of the press and of the politician equally. The approach to solving these problems is really beyond my comprehension and certainly beyond the scope of this discussion.

But I am convinced that the beginning of an approach, the beginning of wisdom in this area has to be the recognition, by us in journalism and by the politician on his side, that there is a common responsibility to the public which these institutions share and which is far more important, far more significant, than the kind of parochial antagonisms that have grown up between us and which divide us so much today.

CHAPTER FOUR

A Publisher's View of Credibility

by

Otis Chandler

Publisher, *Los Angeles Times*

IN THE DECADE that Mr. Otis Chandler has been the publisher of the *Los Angeles Times*, it has become the largest standard-sized metropolitan daily newspaper in the country. Mr. William Schmick, Jr., president of the Baltimore Sunpapers and president of the American Newspaper Publishers Association, in introducing Mr. Chandler at College Park, summed up the developments at the *Times* under Mr. Chandler in this manner:

"I think the best measure of the man is the progress made by the *Los Angeles Times* while under his stewardship. In 1960 the *Los Angeles Times* had three men in Washington; today their 17-man Washington bureau is the second largest bureau in the capital. In addition, they have six other national bureaus spread strategically across the country. Ten years ago the *Los Angeles Times* had one foreign correspondent, and he was headquartered in Paris. Today, the *Times* has 17 foreign bureaus located in world capitals such as London, Moscow, Hong Kong, Beruit. Also, the *Los Angeles Times*, in combination with *The Washington Post*, has a news service with more than 300 clients around the world.

" . . . To sum it up, the *Los Angeles Times* has more lines of advertising and more lines of news than any other newspaper in the world. Actually, I don't know any publisher in the United States who can boast an equal record or a record anywhere approaching that. As you can see, Mr. Chandler is quite a publisher."

Mr. Chandler attended Stanford University and was graduated in 1950 with a B.A. degree in history. He served in the Air Force as a lieutenant before joining the Times-Mirror Co. in 1953. He became publisher of the *Los Angeles Times* in 1960. He is currently vice chairman of the board of the Times-Mirror Co., the parent company.

WE KNOW THERE HAS always been criticism of the press. There has been a question about its credibility for many, many years. For example, the Far Left has criticized the press as being the capitalist press. Today I still hear that, although I hear more from the majority of the Far Right who say that I am, and the *Los Angeles Times* is, influenced by leftists who are leading me and the *Times* down the road toward socialism. It is not this extreme view, however, from the far left or from the far right that concerns me, because I really expect that. What does worry me, and what I refer to when I am talking about a credibility gap today, is a feeling among some parts of the public that they are not getting the facts from the press; that we are not telling it as it is.

There are, I think, several causes for this attitude, not the least of which comes about as the result of television, particularly television news. Television news, in my opinion, has had three important effects on the general credibility of news. On the one hand, television news must, of necessity, be brief. There is, of course, the time problem that they have. It must be highly selective. I also might point out that Los Angeles probably represents the television news wave of the future. For example, in the daily *Los Angeles Times* we list 20 television stations.

There are seven VHF stations in Los Angeles, three UHF's in Los Angeles, five VHF's in San Diego whose signals come into Los Angeles, two more VHF's close by to Los Angeles, one more VHF in Santa Barbara whose signal comes into most of Los Angeles, and one more in Ventura. Now, combined, the nine primary television stations in Los Angeles alone, not San Diego or Santa Barbara, present 91½ hours of news during the five day week. This is evening and morning news, not including special news interruptions, not including interview shows, specials, and not including week-end news. This is twice the news menu presented in New York, which is the second largest television news market.

I am not including radio news time. Radio has two all-news stations 24 hours a day in Los Angeles and frequent newscasts over the other 69 AM and FM stations in the market.

So if there was ever a confrontation between a newspaper and the electronic media in the news side, it is in Los Angeles.

Now back to credibility. Those viewers who place greater reliability on television news often have the illusion that they actually saw it happen on television, because they tend to personally identify with the newscaster, whether it be a Huntley or a Brinkley or a Sevareid.

The question arises, however, for the more sophisticated viewers: what did they really see happen on television last night? What didn't they see that did happen? Certainly a good deal of confusion about the Chicago riots results from the fact that much of what happened throughout the city was never seen or reported.

Television also tends to play stories on the basis of their visibility. If a television station has 500 feet of good film on a story, it is a very tempting thing to want to use that film, particularly if little else is available. When a newspaper comes to you the next morning or the next afternoon with that same story that you saw on television the night before, the newspaper often places a different emphasis on the story because of subsequent developments. There is a tendency for the reader to charge the newspaper, therefore, with bias, because the reader thinks he saw the entire sequence of events on television.

Secondly, when television does record an entire event, such as a press conference, the newspaper may publish only those parts that seem significant. The viewer then wonders why the newspaper doesn't tell the story exactly as television presented it.

A third influence of television news competition is that newspapers are increasingly concentrating on in-depth coverage, interpretative writing. In short, in order to capitalize on the advantage of the printed word, our ability to interpret in depth is paramount.

Another reason for any alleged credibility gap, I think, is a function of the changing nature of the newspaper reporter. It was not too many years ago that most reporters came from ordinary, working-class homes and reflected pretty much the values and prejudices of the mass market. Today, because of the increasing sophistication of the average newspaper reader, because of the trend towards specialized reporting, we are hiring—as many other newspapers are—many reporters from the upper and upper middle classes, men and women who in general are better educated, are more sophisticated, and are certainly paid more than most of our general citizens. They also tend to be more sensitive than the average citizen to the important sociological problems that confront our society today. The net result is, therefore, that what is objective reporting to the reporter may appear biased to those readers who do not share his sensitivity.

Another reason for the credibility gap in the context of this discussion stems from the changing attitudes of political figures and other people who make the news today. As you can well appreciate, there is a new image-consciousness on the part of public officials that pervades our society. Public officials, I think, are far less thick-skinned than they once were. Many important public figures are very sensitive about what people think about them, and they recognize that image is all important to them. That is, their television image. These figures go to great lengths to criticize print when its reportage does not seem as favorable as they had expected.

In California we have two television personalities who are serving in very high public offices, Mayor Yorty of Los Angeles and Governor Reagan who serves in Sacramento as our governor. Both of them have made effective and continual use of television, and they are very critical of the print media—newspapers, magazines and so on—for what they feel is distortion. Now what they feel is distortion means not giving what they feel is proper credit to their image, which looks so good on television. For example, they are very unhappy with us when we, they feel, underestimate the size of the crowds that listen to them in a campaign whistle-stop town. Or, if we said the candidate looked tired, or if we said that his speech was a repeat of what he said ten minutes ago on the last stop—they do not like that. They do not like it, and what do they do about it? They go on television and criticize the newspapers, openly criticize reporters, refuse to grant interviews to reporters—newspaper reporters. They even start their own television shows which Mayor Yorty did in Los Angeles, mainly to find some way of attacking me and the *Los Angeles Times*—he even hired his own political cartoonist, and every Sunday presented his own political cartoon on the publisher of the *Times*.

But I believe more important than all of these factors, which of course do contribute to this claim that there is a credibility gap, is the nature of the news we must report today. We live in an age of incredibly difficult problems, situations which do not lend themselves to simple answers. They are problems the people do not even want to think about, do not want to believe are happening, do not want to believe are true. They are situations which are not credible to the average mind. It is hard to believe for many of our readers and readers across the country that the United States actually has been impossibly involved in a dirty little war in Southeast Asia which we cannot win, and maybe cannot afford to lose, and which is costing us $29 billion a year. It is incredible that a new kind of confrontation politics has enabled, at many campuses and in many areas of the country, small militant minorities to bring one university after another to its knees, to actually so cripple the system that the well-organized and disciplined Far Right can take advantage of the majority establishment backlash against the riots to, in turn, threaten the legitimate rights of the minority students and even the majority students to protest. It is incredible, of course, that our currency—we are the richest nation in the world—is in trouble on the world money market.

Now what can we do about some of these things that I have been talking about? What can the press do about the credibility gap? First, and I think most importantly, we should cover every subject that deserves the attention of a newspaper. I would rather take chances on being controversial than on being dull. We must state our opinions with firmness and strength, and maintain a sense of fairness by telling both sides of every issue, regardless of how controversial that issue is, or regardless of whether it involves an advertiser of our newspaper, regardless of whether it involves friends of the owners of the newspaper, regardless of whether it involves any special interest group. We have to be free and we have to be independent, regardless of how much it hurts us to be so. I do not believe that we should stop reporting the news, negative and frustrating as the news is. I think our mandate is to inform the public, and if in the process we frustrate and anger them that's simply the risk of our business. Because popularity is not our function; telling the truth is.

Nor do I think we should change our in-depth treatment of news in favor of the old styles of journalism. Our job, basically, is to enlarge upon the necessarily fragmentary live reports of radio and television news. Our reporters are capable—they are very intelligent, very imaginative, they have great initiative, they are very idealistic, they are very aggressive, and they are very hard to handle.

The point is that the press today is under attack, and I say "Why not?" Practically all of our institutions today are under attack or under analysis, and I think they should be. Our churches, our schools, the family, law enforcement—so why should the press be treated as a special case?

We all were upset about having some of our reporters arrested and beaten in Chicago. We had three arrested and two beaten, and we were incensed about it, we were unhappy about it, but we didn't editorialize against the Democratic party or against Mayor Daley or against the police chief just because a few of our people were hurt or arrested. It is something with which we have to live and deal. Just as much as our staff in Saigon that covers the war for us is constantly in danger, those who go in to cover a riot area are in danger.

An independent and free press is essential to the survival of this country. It would be indeed tragic if the press were to be so sensitive and so concerned about its own image that it were to capitulate or surrender its absolutely essential role of giving the people the hard facts of life today.

Once we start worrying too often or too deeply about what certain individuals and what certain groups think about us, then we might start selling our souls for the sake of expediency. I suggest if that day ever comes, then the press has had it.

CHAPTER FIVE

The Administration's View of Press and Politics

by

Herbert G. Klein

Director of Communications, The White House

AS DIRECTOR OF COMMUNICATIONS for the executive branch of government, Mr. Herbert G. Klein is specifically charged with overseeing the flow of information from all departments of President Richard Nixon's Administration. Political reporter David Broder wrote in 1969 of Mr. Klein and his position: "He and his aides are — as promised — serving as catalysts for the Administration members who are hesitant or uncertain how to improve the flow of information from their departments. Klein has also made himself an effective intermediary for members of the press who run into problems covering the Administration." The Broder article pointed out that the consequence has been less "bad reporting," an open atmosphere, and no attempt to conceal differences of opinion within the Administration.

Mr. Klein has had a long relationship with newspapers. It began after his graduation from the University of California in 1940, and was interrupted by wartime service with the Navy. Since the war, he has worked as news editor of the *Alhambra* (Calif.) *Post-Advocate*, Washington correspondent for the Copley Newspapers, and editor of the *San Diego Union*. As editor of the *Union*, he gained a national reputation as a spokesman for freedom of information. Since 1952, he has interrupted newspaper work five times to join the campaigns of Mr. Nixon.

TODAY, I THINK it is more important than at any time in American history for the politician and for the journalist to be particularly articulate, to be able to explain to the American people the great complexities that confront this nation and the world.

Whether he be in newspaper, radio, or television, the journalist's responsibilities today are so much greater than at any time in the past that it makes it a particularly difficult matter to handle. Yet, the responsibility is such that, unless we do a good job in the field of journalism, we are not going to be able to carry out the total duties of the press in its relationship to the American voter and citizen.

Look, for example at the problems that confronted the President as he took office, and you can see the complexities it brings to the journalist who's trying to cover them. When the President came into office, we were confronted, of course, with the war in Vietnam, with a near-war in the Middle East, with a need to cement our relationship with our own allies in Europe, with the need to build some kind of a dialogue with the Soviet Union as the major power on the other side, and with all the other complex problems in the various parts of the world. On the domestic front, there were the urban problems, the problems in the air, the need to further develop our own national resources so as to provide for the needs of a growing population, the problems of racial disorder, the disorders on the campus, the problems of hunger and malnutrition, and of growing welfare rolls.

When you look at this from the standpoint of the press in covering those who are making these decisions, it is a difficult thing because no decision made today can be other than a complex one. For example, when you explain a new program on tax reform, it is necessary that you have skilled journalists who not only say that the President today announced a tax reform package and it contained these things, but who can also see accurately and interpret what these things mean and how they apply to you as an individual, or what they do to the economy or to your own income.

One of the major things which we have enacted in the Nixon Administration to try to attack the problem frontally has been the concept of what the President had in mind in what we call "open government."

In doing this, we went back to analyze our experiences in providing press coverage in campaigns and during the time he was vice president. We tried to analyze what had worked most effectively in meeting the interpretation of complex government.

I talked with four of the former press secretaries, for all of whom I have a great deal of respect. These were Jim Hagerty, who I think was the best we have ever had, and three other excellent ones—Mr. Pierre Salinger, Mr. George Christian, and Mr. Bill Moyers. We asked them, "How do you relay the growing number of events in government?" and "What were the problems you faced in getting things out and keeping things in?"

We also looked at the experience we had during the last election campaign. I have served in about five campaigns and as I came back into this campaign last year, I felt we could do a better job for the campaign, and also for the public, if we divided the press responsibilities so that there was a traveling press aide, Mr. Ron Ziegler, who would travel with the candidate.

My responsibility then would be in charge of the total press coverage and I would work out of our New York headquarters so I could participate in policy decisions and could keep information flowing to the airplane, as well as working with others who could speak articulately on behalf of the campaign itself.

The decision was made late in November that we would follow basically this technique in the new Administration, so the news operation in the government today breaks down roughly this way.

Now, Mr. Ron Ziegler—who I think, incidentally, is one of the brightest young men to come into the government; he has just reached age thirty—is the press secretary to the President, and as such handles the daily briefings for the press. In other words, twice a day he goes before the press, answers their questions, relays the activities of the President, and makes the announcements on behalf of the President himself.

In my own role as the director of communications, I am charged with information policies of the overall government and as such I sit in on the various policy meetings in the White House, the Cabinet, the National Security Council, and other major staff meetings.

Members of my office and myself work in constant liaison with the departments of government, ranging from cabinet departments to the smaller departments which from time to time assume major importance.

Our effort in doing this is to enable these departments to get more facts to the American public. In doing so, we run some risks because the more people we have speaking for the government, the more we can have differences. But we feel that the differences which might be expressed are less important than the value we have gained by getting out more information.

The President has taken the same direct attitude and my job is made possible because of his strength behind me. Our attitude is that we want the cabinet officers to be in various parts of the country explaining to the American people what happens in their departments. We want them on television as much as possible. We want them to grant interviews, press conferences, things of this kind. Our theory is that the more the American people know about government and the more they know about the functions of their own governmental affairs, the better the government will be able to function and the more believable it will be.

In terms of the role of the press as it covers the government, you have got another variety of things. Most of us see the glamorous side of the press in Washington where we watch the reporters who cover the White House and then go on television and report. Or, we read stories in the newspapers from the bureau chiefs and those who are on the all-star level.

But it is our belief that a great number of the experts who cover departments can do an excellent job in interpreting the intricate affairs of government if they are given better opportunity by having the major news actually emanate from the Department of Health, Education, and Welfare, or the Department of Housing and Urban Development, or the Department of Agriculture, or whatever. Those who know those skills best then will be writing a great number of the stories. In the past most of the so-called "goodies" were issued through the White House so that attention would be on the President himself. We feel that the American public welcomes a team report. Our effort then is to provide a broad team.

In this process I think that the press has a role of representing the American public. In many ways a press conference is the American equivalent of having the prime minister come before Parliament in the British system and undergo the questioning of the members of Parliament.

In this case the theory of the American process is that the person asking questions is representing you as an American citizen and he seeks the information so that it can be transmitted to the general public.

One of the press problems, I think, that has arisen in recent years is the growth of television question-and-answer shows. Too often reporters have become showmen who want to ask a question that might trip the person, rather than a question that might be aimed at getting the actual news. I have found little evidence of this during this Administration, but over a period of years it has been a problem that has grown, and I suspect it will come back again from time to time. I think the role of the reporter is to be an anonymous questioner, not the person who is standing up to gain public attention because the television camera is on, or one who gets public attention because he was able to gain some kind of a concession—which isn't necessarily the accurate fact—by a question that had some trick end to it.

Certainly the duty of the reporter is to ask hard questions. The questions are not always pleasant, and they shouldn't be. And it is the duty of the politician, in my opinion, to answer the questions as directly as possible, whenever it is possible. It is our attitude that military security is an area that has to be guarded and that everyone must agree that the answers cannot be given in certain security areas.

There are other areas where, if one doesn't have the answer yet, it is better not to try to fake it but to honestly admit that the full story isn't known.

A lot of questions have been raised in recent years as to what effect the editorials of the nation's press have on the politicians in Washington. It is my feeling that the editorials overall—when you look at them on a national basis—probably have less effect today than they had in the years past.

I suppose if you are a Republican there is some disadvantage to this, because while a majority of the newspapers have supported Republican candidates editorially most of the reporters have been Democratically oriented, and so the press reports versus the editorial page seemingly favor the other side. But I wouldn't want to leave the impression that a reporter's political leanings necessarily influence his story. In my opinion, the majority of the press reports today are fair and this is not the case.

One of the overlooked aspects of the editorials, though, is in terms of the continued strength of editorials in the smaller newspapers, the community newspapers, because of the personal effect where the editor himself is known to many of his readers. These, I believe, have a tremendous impact on their own communities.

I also believe that in areas where you have great numbers of opinionmakers gathered, as in Washington or New York, or perhaps Los Angeles, San Francisco, or Chicago, the editorials there have a far greater strength than do those in other similar communities of equal size in other parts of the country. Thus, the editorials that appear in the

Washington papers do have an effect on the opinions of those in the Congress. They are read carefully by those in the Administration and I am sure that they are taken into consideration for the formulation of opinions in all parts of government.

I think, to look at it another way, when you get to a close decision, such as the debate over the ABM Safeguard system, editorial opinions in certain areas may have an effect on those who would sway one way or the other in a particularly close vote.

Editorials serve several other audiences. I believe the American people look to editorials and columns for an explanation of what the issues of the debate are. Beyond the American public, another area where I think editorials have impact is with foreign audiences. Certainly the Vietcong, in weighing the effect of a policy speech on Vietnam and weighing the support of the President in this very critical program, examine what the American opinion is of this speech and they examine it in the easiest form, in terms of the editorials. They also examine it in the form of letters of comment and other aspects of opinion as they are manifested. So, wide support for the President's program will be a helpful aspect in terms of negotiations.

One other aspect of the public area that I

would like to touch on is that in this particular administration we intend to put great stress upon the relationship between the individual and his government. We believe that the time is right to involve more people in their own communities. I think a great number of you young people have shown the way in this by your own interest in the welfare of your country and the welfare of your people— whether it be in terms of hunger, whether it be in terms of civil rights, whatever it may be. I believe that this is indicated at your age and it is translated into all ages. There is a renewed desire of the American people to take a greater part in community activity. We can put forth a number of programs but they will be effective only if the press itself is interested in them and makes the possibilities evident to the American people. Today's press faces a challenge from all sides. It faces the problems from the politicians who feel that it is unfair, who have been critical of it from both the left and from the right. It faces the problem of believability by the American public. Too many people today say they cannot believe what they read in the newspaper, or that they do not believe what they hear on radio or TV. Each time this is said it undermines the very basic strength of the freedom of the press, because a free press survives only so long as the American people have the will and desire to allow it to survive, to support it as a free institution and to fight against inroads of those on the political side who might wish to put new regulations against those institutions of the press.

You see your own evidences of someone who takes a small step here and a small step there toward further regulation of a free press. It is my opinion that the press has a credibility problem of its own in terms of convincing the American people that it is telling the full story, in terms of convincing the American people that freedom of the press is worth the price.

Our job in government is also one of convincing people that they can believe in the government as it now exists. So, in many ways we have a parallel problem.

If the American people lose faith in the credibility of government—and they have over a period of years—and if this deteriorates further, it endangers the basic form of government we have. If the people can't believe what they hear from their top officials, if the world can't believe what it hears from American officials, no longer will there be faith in the ability of any administration to serve the people.

So, I think that the efforts of the press in terms

of gaining a reputation by performance, in how it interprets the news and how it presents the news, and the efforts of government in regaining the confidence of the American people by speaking the truth, by truly facing up to the facts whether they are good or bad, run a parallel course of great importance to the future of this nation.

I have great confidence that with the renewed vigor we will put into the government, with the quality of the press that I see across the country, that this is a danger period that will be overcome. It is my opinion that in the four or eight years ahead, if we do the job we are charged to do, the American people will again have the faith they should have in their own American institutions.

If we fail to do this, I believe we will have failed in our task and it will be the responsibility of the American people to make the kind of change that is necessary to give someone else an opportunity to reach this goal.

I believe we will succeed.

CHAPTER SIX

Political Reporting: The Criteria of Selection

by

Philip Potter

Washington Bureau Chief, The *Baltimore Sun*

PHILIP POTTER is chief of the Washington bureau of the *Baltimore Sun*, a position he has held since 1964. He also serves the *Sun* as its White House correspondent.

Mr. Potter began work in journalism in 1934 when he became an Associated Press correspondent immediately after his graduation from the University of Minnesota. In 1936, he became managing editor of *The Rapid City* (S.D.) *Daily Journal,* remaining there until 1941 when he joined the staff of the *Baltimore Sun.*

After a period as city editor of the *Sun,* Mr. Potter was assigned to the China-India-Burma theater as a war correspondent. He remained in the Far East after the war to cover the American occupation of Korea and the Marshall mission to China, then returned home to take a position in the *Sun's* Washington bureau. A year later he was again a foreign correspondent.

He worked the major stories of that post-war period—the Berlin airlift, the civil war in Greece, the Arab-Israeli conflict in Palestine, and then was assigned to the Korean warfront where he was wounded by machine gun fire.

During the remainder of the 1950's, Mr. Potter covered national issues as a member of the *Sun's* Washington bureau—and made frequent trips to Asia. In 1961, he became the first chief of the New Delhi bureau of the *Sun,* and remained in India through 1962. In 1964, he was assigned to Washington.

PRIME MINISTER DISRAELI once said of the British press that it is not only free, but powerful.

That can probably be said of the press in any democratic non-totalitarian country where editors and reporters are free to determine what they will publish. But it probably is truer of the American press than of that in any other country because of our constitutional arrangements. For one thing, freedom of the press is part of our Bill of Rights and it is zealously guarded by the press and the courts. For another, the separation of powers between the executive, legislative, and judicial branches and the fact that our president does not report directly to Congress, as the British prime minister and his cabinet report to the House of Commons for public questioning, lays on the American press an uncommon intelligence function. It not only is a medium by which the various branches communicate with the public but with each other.

As Douglass Cater wrote in *Power in Washington*, the power of the press to determine what is news can be decisive, even reshaping the priorities of government itself. "News," he wrote, "is a fundamental force in the struggle to govern. Each day hundreds of thousands of words are spoken, tens of dozens of events occur. The press and other media perform the arduous task of sorting out and assigning priorities to these words and events. This capacity to choose with speed and brevity which stories command widespread attention and which go unnoticed constitutes a power far more formidable than the purely editorial preferences of the press."

There is a good deal of dispute as to whether the press and other mass media fulfill this role with the sense of responsibility and objectivity it would seem to require. In fact, one could say of the American press what Justice Jackson said of the Supreme Court, "It's not that we are final because we are infallible; we are infallible because we are final." It is hardly surprising that those subjected to press scrutiny—those who seek office and those who gain it—are acutely sensitive to the press role and what might be called government by publicity.

Although the press can be and has been manipulated by clever politicians, it usually has not been for long. Many made by the press have been unmade by it a bit later. Senator Joseph McCarthy of Wisconsin who acquired a formidable public following in the early 1950's is a clear-cut example. For four years he used his senatorial immunity from libel to put out pseudo-news exaggerating the penetration of Democratic and even Republican administrations by communists. His releases were so adroitly timed that most newsmen, and the sharply-competing wire services in particular, seldom had time to go into the import or validity of his charges. Before one was exposed as inaccurate, he had made another that had captured the headlines.

But the press and other mass media which he used to build himself up eventually brought him down by exposing the misuse of his power to seek favors for an Army private who had been an inconsequential member of his staff, his chief duty as a millionaire hotel man being to pick up the checks when the Senator and his entourage ran up a bill at a posh Washington or New York restaurant or nightspot. The press was more at home bringing this pseudo-investigator down than in elevating him to public stature. As Marshall McLuhan wrote a few years ago, the American press is happiest fulfilling its function "when revealing the seamy side." Real news is bad news, bad news about somebody or bad news for somebody.

Only the advertisements always have good news for the readers. That, of course, is as true of political advertising as of any other. Practitioners of the political art—and it is an art and not a science—have learned to put Madison Avenue techniques to good use in selling themselves or their programs.

Newspapermen, as well as the electorate, get taken in by such advertising. But once a man gets into the office he seeks, whether he is president or governor, county commissioner or justice of the peace, there comes a time of reckoning.

As Leo Rosten wrote a quarter century ago: "Newspapermen greet (a newly-elected president) with the hope that here at last is the great man incarnate. The great man's talents are sung, oversung in the struggle for journalistic existence. Then 'incidents' occur, a political compromise of not admirable hue, a political setback, attacks come from the opposition, the newspapermen begin to see feet of clay. They have been taken in, their faith has been outraged. How did they ever 'fall for that stuff?' . . . Other newsmen, columnists, editors, publishers cry that the press corps has been hamstrung by phrases. The correspondents are hurt. They are irritated. And they feel guilty. The breaking of the myth begins by the very men who erected it."

How do we go about performing the function of informing the American people whom they ought to or ought not to elect to the nation's highest office? The process is not very mysterious or very profound. From a staff of about a dozen in the Washington bureau of the *Sun,* we assign one man to more or less full-time coverage of national politics. In a national election year most of the staff in Washington is so engaged, and extra reporters are borrowed from the Baltimore office, usually men with experience in Maryland politics and statehouse coverage.

One of the keenest political writers on the newspaper is Charles Whiteford, who not only knows all there is to know about Maryland politics, but covers national conferences of governors and often has been in the South on racial problems. He was a natural for assignment to cover the Southern region last year, giving special attention to George C. Wallace's bid for the presidency.

Another from the Baltimore staff was Gene Oishi, who had covered Governor Spiro Agnew for two years and was a natural choice to follow the GOP vice-presidential candidate around the country in the fall campaign.

A third man from Baltimore, Theo Lippman, was assigned to Senator Edmund S. Muskie, vice-presidential candidate on the Democratic ticket.

In the meantime, the Washington staff's Ernest B. Furgurson, then chief political writer and now an editorial page columnist, had been covering the primaries from New Hampshire to California, occasionally aided by others from Washington who were assigned primarily to the leading contenders wherever they appeared.

As Washington bureau chief I kept an eye on President Johnson until he dropped out of presidential contention on March 31. I made the first coast-to-coast swing with Senator Robert F. Kennedy and spent time before the conventions with Senator McCarthy, Richard Nixon, Vice President Humphrey and George C. Wallace.

The newspaper sent large staffs from Washington and Baltimore to each of the major national conventions, headed by the managing editor, the editor in charge of the editorial pages, and the Washington bureau chief. In Chicago we had two men, for instance, watching nothing but street demonstrations and police activity.

In the fall campaign we used both a regional and a man-to-man coverage. Men were assigned full-time to both presidential candidates and their running mates. And there were regional men—one in the South, one in the West, and one in the East— who watched the presidential scene in their own areas—we didn't have a full-time man on Wallace— and kept an eye on key congressional races. Vacations went by the board for the entire Washington staff until after the national election.

In off-year elections we use the regional system to cover key senatorial contests and races for the House, while our chief political writer roves the country all the time covering by-elections and keeping an eye on potential presidential candidates.

These full-time political writers, as David Broder noted in *Washington Monthly*, probably number no more than two dozen men and women. There is one for each of the wire services, the three networks and the major papers like *The Washington Post, New York Times, Baltimore Sun*, and the *Christian Science Monitor*. But altogether no more than 25 or so devote full-time to political writing.

They constitute, of course, a very powerful screening committee in determining who is and who is not presidential timber. They record the contenders' speeches, usually with considerable accuracy despite Mr. Nixon's famous complaint after his losing 1962 gubernatorial race in California that he wished newspapers would "put one lonely reporter on the campaign that will report what the candidate says now and then."

They also try to determine who he sees and why, what deals he is making, and the mood of the electorate and its attitude toward the candidates. They pay keen attention to the national opinion polls. They interview politicians, party leaders, leading citizens, and occasionally poll the man-on-the-street. They are talent scouts, handicappers, and, as David Broder wrote, some of them become self-constituted public defenders or, alternatively, assistant campaign managers for candidates that they happen to fancy. Martin F. Nolan of the *Boston Globe* once compared national political reporters to a band of traveling drama critics, covering the new political acts at their out-of-town openings, and their reports, like those in *Variety*, frequently making or breaking the men they cover, as happened to Michigan's George Romney.

Despite all efforts to be neutral and objective, newsman are human beings and political writers no less so than others. As Broder put it, selectivity is the essence of all contemporary journalism, and selectivity implies criteria. Criteria depend on value judgments which, he said, are fancy words for opinions, prejudices, and preconceptions. There is no neutral journalism.

The political journalist's function as handicapper or forecaster of the success or failure of this or that politician probably is his most controversial job. For one thing, an unfavorable forecast can cost a contender for office a serious loss in contributions. Vice President Humphrey's managers said last fall that unfavorable public opinion polls after the Chicago convention made it very difficult for them to finance his campaign.

But every country has its forecasters. When I was running the *Sun's* bureau in New Delhi back in

1961, the astrologers, sadhus, swamis, and other assorted stargazers who carry out communications in that country foresaw a February calamity but they maintained they could ward it off with prayers and sacrificial rites if they got enough money from the people.

The money poured in, especially from the women. Of course nothing happened. The stargazers proclaimed their success in warding off calamity. But some got what was coming to them. In one little suburb of Agra near New Delhi, for instance, three sadhus who had persuaded a number of women to part with gold and cash as offerings to ward off evil were stopped as they carried their loot away by male relatives of the credulous females. They beat up the sadhus and forced them to return the valuables to the women.

Perhaps American journalistic soothsayers would be more careful in their predictions if they faced a similar ordeal.

CHAPTER SEVEN

Politics, BlAcks, ANd thE PRESS

by

William Raspberry

Columnist, The Washington Post

AS THE AUTHOR of "Potomac Watch," a column appearing four times a week in *The Washington Post,* Mr. William Raspberry has become well known for his knowledge of the urban poor. In a city where the population is more than two-thirds Negro, his column is concerned, naturally enough, with problems like race relations, poverty, welfare, drug addiction, and urban crime. Mr. Raspberry, however, does more than report and complain about problems. His columns offer thoughtful, incisive analyses of causes and advance reasonable, progressive points of view for their clarification and solution. His column provides a unique and valuable point of view for various audiences — Negroes from the gold coast of northwest Washington to the slum areas of the inner city, concerned whites in the city and suburbs, and the District and federal governments.

Mr. Raspberry is a graduate of Indiana Central College. He worked during the late 1950's as a reporter for the *Indianapolis Recorder,* a Negro weekly. He came to Washington in 1960 as a public information officer for the U. S. Army. Mr. Raspberry was hired by *The Washington Post* in 1962 as a teletype operator and moved through positions of library assistant, police and court reporter, copy editor, and general assignment reporter to become assistant city editor. In 1966, he became the writer of the regular feature "Potomac Watch." His 1965 coverage of the Watts riot brought him the Capital Press Club's "Journalist of the Year" award. And, in 1967, he received the Front Page Award from the Washington-Baltimore Newspaper Guild for best interpretative reporting.

WHEN THE RIOTING became a summer institution, it made newspapers aware of how long and
how completely they had been ignoring the black
community.

Traditionally, the general press had covered
the ghetto only in so far as it affected the white community, and so we had a situation where ghettos
across the country were burning and nobody knew
why because nobody knew what the area had been
like before—partly because newspapers didn't care,
because they assumed their readers didn't care, and
partly because most of the big city newspapers had
few black reporters who could lend their insights.

I was pulled off the desk to go to Watts to cover
the rioting there in 1965. There's an interesting reason for that. We had been relying on the *Los Angeles Times* to keep us posted on what was going on
out there. The *Post* and the *Times* have a joint news
service and we sort of scratch each other's backs.

But at the time Watts exploded, the *Times*, although it is one of the nation's leading newspapers,
was caught absolutely flat-footed. The reporters for
the *Los Angeles Times*, as reporters always do when
big stories break, rushed to the newspaper's morgue
to see what the newspaper had said about Watts up
to this point. They were dismayed to find not a single clip on Watts. Not even a file. For the *Los An-*

geles Times, Watts simply had not existed until it exploded in August of 1965. So, the *Post* sent me to Los Angeles to help us catch up on what was going on, since white reporters were unable to get into the riot area.

The *Times,* and newspapers across the country, learned some things out of that embarrassment of being caught so flat-footed. Nearly every big city newspaper became rather painfully aware that it knew nothing, virtually nothing, about its own ghetto areas.

It also brought home to black people and to poor people that they could command the attention of the press. And they found that this attention could lead to some positive gains for them, through efforts at the local, state, and federal levels to do something about their plight.

Until then, I think there had never been any real belief that they could win the attention of the press and the community. They found out that they could, and I think that is one of the reasons why rioting flourished. It got to a point where riots or threats of disorder or demonstrations that had the prospect of getting out of hand always got the press out there. And for the first time we started reading and hearing about some of the grievances poor people had. There was, I suspect, a good deal of over-reaction to it, of which black people took advantage, of course.

Newsmen, who heretofore had been acting as though poor black people didn't exist, started to act as though if you were poor and black you couldn't say anything wrong. Every utterance had some essential kernel of truth. It spilled over beyond the press. I recall sitting in on poverty meetings, for example, where you had the so-called indigenous poor on the same boards with ordinary middle class types and the poor representative could say the most stupid thing in the world and the middle class people would sit around and say how beautiful it was and how it just summed up everything so perfectly. We still have a lot of that, both in the press and out.

The primary motives for increasing the coverage of the black community were almost totally selfish, at least at the beginning. As every major city came to realize that it, too, could have a riot, no self-respecting big city newspaper wanted to be caught in the position in which the *Los Angeles Times* had been caught.

First, they started looking for black reporters. Then they started paying a little less attention to the "certified Negro leaders," whose organizations had largely lost touch, if they had ever been in touch, with the poor, the slum poor. They started searching out the indigenous black leadership that seemed to be speaking for the ghetto poor. And naturally enough, when this started to happen the press was accused of creating such incendiary leaders as Stokely Carmichael and Rap Brown. Well, of course, the press did create them, if by that you mean that their names would not be known without the involvement of the press. But there is no gainsaying that radical, militant blacks, who the press created, were in fact speaking for a lot of the poor in the ghettos across the country.

And, in my view, the press would have been derelict to ignore their utterances. Now I know that people like Whitney Young, for example, have described Stokely Carmichael's following as 5,500 people—500 black people and 5,000 reporters. In a sense it is true, if you are talking about organized memberships in organizations headed by people like Carmichael. But the views they hold, the anger they express, their condemnation of what life in the central cities is all about, I think strikes a responsive chord in a frighteningly large number of the slum poor.

The press is also charged, as a result of this new interest, with paying too much attention to the newly-organized poor and the black militants and thereby distorting its coverage of black people generally. Now that is a fairly serious charge and it may be justified. It at least warrants some exploration. Newspapers, and now television stations and radio stations, are wrestling with this very question. It comes about partly because of the nature of news. If news is the unusual occurrence, the extraordinary event, then it does tend to distort unless the reader knows something about the ordinary people involved. For example, a story about a suburban housewife who goes berserk and does something weird—murders her family or whatever—is news. Obviously when she does this she becomes news. But the readers already know lots and lots of ordinary suburban housewives, so they are able to fit the eccentric one into some sort of context.

If we apply the same guidelines to a coverage of the Negro community and write about the ones who do something extraordinarily good or extraordinarily bad and you don't know anything about ordinary black people, you don't have the context in which to fit the extraordinary ones. The result, of course, is distortion.

The phrase is, you know, the newspapers always cover the freaks, and this is true. And newspapers, although they have never had to build the context for any other group, are now thinking that maybe they'll have to for black people, just to avoid this kind of distortion.

It has not worked out very satisfactorily to report only on those people who do extraordinary things that make news. Because, as I said, that leads to distortion. On the other hand, it is not very satisfactory to write patronizingly about it—you know, to take a white reader on a tour of an ordinary black community as though you were taking him on an excursion to Somalia or some place. I don't think that any newspaper that I know of has really come up with a satisfactory solution yet.

The other charge I hear fairly often is that if the Kerner Commission was right, for example, and if America is a racist system, rushing headlong into two separate societies and the press is a reflection of this society—and maybe the press ought to be a reflection of the society it covers, I don't know—where does this fit in the press—is the press itself racist? Does the press have a responsibility beyond simply reflecting the society? Does it have some responsibility to exert some leadership? If so, in what directions? Is the press leading this rush into two separate societies? Or toward unity? I honestly don't know.

In general, the responsibility of the black press is the responsibility of the press generally. It is to tell—to keep the readers informed about those things that interest them. The black press, naturally, is supposed to be telling black people about things that should be of interest to the black community. The fact is that it has not for a good long while done an adequate job of it. There are a lot of reasons for that.

The black press is almost always a weekly press and for as long as the general press, the white press, was ignoring the black community, it could do a sort of "catch-up" every week on what had happened of interest to the black community.

It had initially dedicated itself to working itself out of existence. If it could force the attention of the white press on black people, then there would be no need for a special press. It succeeded to a great extent, but, of course, it won't go out of business now. It has become a business and it has become a not very successful one. It is mostly hanging on.

It has very little income because with advertising they have difficulty demonstrating that they have readers that the daily press doesn't have; therefore, the advertiser might think his dollar is better spent in the daily press.

So, when you have a low budget, you have to pay low salaries and you find yourself hiring would-be journalists, rather than journalists. And as soon as they become any good, you find them being lured away by the general press with more lucrative salaries. I think for most black newspapers I have seen, the future is very, very dim. Some newspapers are trying to improve their coverage and to improve the quality of their reportage. Some are doing it fairly successfully. Some are finding it pays to pay better salaries to try to hold the young reporters they have developed.

I think there are a lot of Negro reporters now working for the general press who would be willing to take a small pay cut to go back to work for the Negro press because they think they have some special insights and special inputs that could be of value.

CHAPTER EIGHT

The Influence of Polling on Politics and the Press

by
George Gallup, Jr.
President, American Institute of Public Opinion

GEORGE GALLUP, JR., has been associated with the American Institute of Public Opinion since taking his degree at Princeton University in 1953. In 1966, he replaced his father, Dr. George Gallup, as president of the American Institute of Public Opinion with the elder Gallup becoming board chairman. In the years previous to assuming that position, he had been editor of the Gallup Poll and has served as a liaison between the home office in Princeton, New Jersey, and Gallup International—an organization with Gallup-affiliated companies in 26 countries.

The American Institute of Public Opinion was established in 1935 by Mr. Gallup's father, who had developed opinion research techniques during and after his study at the University of Iowa.

Mr. Gallup has published numerous studies on the voting behavior of groups within our society. He is a member of the American Association of Public Opinion Research. He attended Oxford after completing academic work at Princeton.

POLLS, BOTH PUBLIC AND PRIVATE, accounted for some of the biggest surprises last year in a surprising election year. George Romney dropped out of the presidential race because his private polls showed him losing badly to Nixon. Robert Kennedy entered the race when polls convinced him that he could beat Lyndon Johnson in the California primary. In renouncing a second term, Johnson was influenced by a Gallup Poll that showed that only 26 per cent of the people approved his handling of the Vietnam war.

Criticism is sometimes heard that the president and others in high office "pay too much attention to polls." In my opinion, this is not an intelligent criticism since usually it springs from a misunderstanding of the nature of polls and the purposes they serve. Polling organizations are fact-finding agencies. They serve the same function for government leaders as the intelligence division of the Army does for the Army staff. The intelligence division does not make the final decisions about the conduct of the battle; it merely supplies information which enables the commanding general to make better decisions. Poll findings are of the same order. They help government leaders make better decisions. The president, as in the case of the commanding general, is free to use this evidence or to ignore it. In the end he must follow his own best judgment, but that judgment is likely to be improved and not harmed by *more* rather than *less* information about the state of public opinion. To seek information, therefore, from polls that have established their reliability is not a weakness, it is not evidence of indecision or lack of leadership—it is a sign of intelligence.

The criticism that political leaders pay too much attention to polls is only one of many charges that have been leveled at polls in the latest presidential as well as in earlier presidential races.

We are accused of interviewing too few people, of being unable to get honest answers, of "cooking" our results, of timing their publication to serve some end, of "loading" our questions, of creating a "bandwagon effect."

In every presidential election year "open season" on polltakers is declared, with the shooting usually coming from those who don't like the findings. People across the nation write or telephone us to remind us of 1948, to ask why they haven't been interviewed, or just to give us a piece of their minds.

One person during the campaign wrote my father: "Discontinue this very crooked manner of earning your livelihood, even if it means selling pencils or peanuts, as it will be something earned in an honest manner."

Another of our "fans" reminded us of 1948 and wrote: "Dr. Gallup, you hid in the tall timbers once—you shouldn't mind doing it again."

In this quadrennial storm of abuse we cannot look for refuge with the nation's columnists—at least some of them. I suspect that one reason for their sharp attacks is that we take a little of the fun out of their job of sniffing the political winds.

One of the favorite pitches of political columnists has been to warn their readers that people just won't talk to interviewers—and if they do, they won't tell an interviewer the truth. In this election, they said that people wouldn't admit they were voting for Wallace. Four years ago they said the same thing about Goldwater supporters.

But the simple truth is that people don't lie. If they did, then polling would be impossible and producing an accurate estimate of the vote would be a matter of sheer luck.

Election polling presents tremendous headaches for polltakers. For example, we have to find out not only which candidates are preferred, but how many persons are likely to go to the polls. And where does the "undecided" vote go?

We sympathize with Dr. Henry Durant, head of the Gallup Poll in Great Britain, when in addressing a group of university students in that country, he advised would-be pollsters to think again:

It's the most stupid job you can ever take up no matter how hard you try to find a worse one. If you get the election result right, everyone takes it for granted. If you get it wrong, you are standing out alone and utterly naked, and there's nothing you can do about it.

Election polling, though extremely difficult, has served an important end—it has helped greatly to develop sophisticated research methods and it does provide the "acid" test of a polling organization's capabilities.

That progress has been made through the years in improving polling methods and procedures can be seen in the fact that the average deviation for the nine national elections covered by the Gallup Poll between 1936 and 1952 was 3.7 percentage points, and 1.4 for the eight national elections between 1954 and 1968.

We are proud to say that this record of accuracy has never been equaled in U.S. polling history. In fact, no other national poll has produced more accurate findings in any *one* of the *nine* elections since 1952.

This high level of accuracy is the result of painstaking effort in developing a scientific, workable method. In every election, experience gained is carefully analyzed. On this basis, we try to incorporate new refinements to help improve some aspect of the total system. Findings are produced by the method without subjective judgment or interpretation.

In speaking of election surveys, let me say that we are not eager to have a repetition of 1948 when we stopped polling too soon, missed the trend to Truman, and became perfect bait for the wits and pundits that year.

One story went around that the Gallup Poll had changed it telephone number to "Truman-Won-Oh-Oh-Oh." Someone else said that 1948 was the year the Gallup Poll "committed Deweycide." Another humorist said that "Truman won in a walk, but lost in a Gallup."

A booklet found its way to my father's desk, with the title, *What Dr. Gallup Knows About Polls*. When it was opened, it revealed nothing but blank pages.

The question asked most often is: "Why haven't I been interviewed?" The question asked us second most frequently is: "What happened in 1948?"

Phyllis McGinley, the poetess, has complained: "Before the untold multitudes *trample* me, won't someone please *sample* me?" Such frustration is apparent in a recent letter from a Syracuse, New York, woman:

Dear Dr. Gallup: Back in the thirties I wrote to you and said that I had never known anyone, who knew anyone, who had ever been queried for a Gallup Poll. I waited patiently to be interviewed for several years. Now, many years, three children, one Ph.D., a number of states later, I still have never known anyone, who knew anyone, who had been questioned for a Gallup Poll. And this includes myself.

The Gallup Poll—like the Harris Survey—is a *published* poll as opposed to a *private* poll. The Gallup Poll has never engaged in work for a political party or candidate, in order to preserve our record for impartiality.

The Gallup Poll is published twice weekly in 140 newspapers representing all shades of political belief. Close to 5,000 individual reports on a tremendous variety of subjects have been sent to client newspapers since our founding in 1935.

The *private* polls are commissioned by candidates and their supporters and are carefully studied by campaign managers and other political insiders for clues to voters' attitudes and likely behavior.

More than 200 firms—large and small, regional and national—were active in political polling during the 1968 campaign. It is estimated that more than half of U.S. congressional candidates made use of some kind of poll during the last election, while the figure was much higher in the case of U.S. senatorial candidates.

No firm figures are available as to the amount of money spent on political polls for candidates in the last election, but one estimate puts the figure at three million.

As public opinion analyst Charles Roll of *Political Surveys and Analyses* points out, one of the long-range effects of John F. Kennedy's successful campaign for the presidency in 1960 has been the great impact which the privately commissioned poll has on the political world. President Kennedy, unlike other candidates up to that time, made no secret of the extensive use he made of the polling technique as an important tool of his campaign. As a result, in steadily increasing numbers, candidates, wealthy friends of candidates, political parties at all levels and of both major varieties, labor unions, and lobbying organizations, among others, have sought out the political poll-taker.

It will come as a surprise to most, however, that Kennedy was not the first politician—nor even the first presidential candidate—to commission his own poll data. There were many people in public life who made use of survey research prior to 1960.

Mrs. Alex Miller in 1932 was elected the first

woman secretary of the state of Iowa. This distinction, however, is dwarfed by another. In the process of seeking this office, she probably became the first candidate for political office ever to have the benefit of the special insight provided by polling data. To test her chances of winning, a young man applied to the Iowa electorate for political purposes the same sampling techniques he had developed as a Ph.D. candidate to find out from a newspaper's readership just which news stories and advertisements were being read. He found she had a good chance of winning, pinpointing, as it were, the approaching Democratic sweep in Republican Iowa. The young man was her son-in-law and my father, Dr. George Gallup, who four years later contradicted the then-respected *Literary Digest* by predicting the reelection of Franklin Roosevelt to a second presidential term.

This President, as it turned out, was the first high elected official to commission survey research to determine public attitudes. Dr. Hadley Cantril tells of Roosevelt's interest beginning the spring of 1940 in obtaining trend information on public attitudes toward aiding the allies in general and on specific measures prior to our entry into World War II. The first presidential hopeful to use polls was Thomas Dewey. In 1940, Gerald Lambert, a retired industrialist, sponsored surveys for the then district attorney of Manhattan primarily to raise the level of acceptability of Dewey's speeches in his preconvention campaign for the Republican nomination. Dewey was successful in several primaries in which the survey results were applied, but lost to the Willkie-blitz at the convention.

The chief value of private polls is not finding out who's going to win, but "What's bothering voters?" These polls also help candidates find out how they can improve their image. Still another purpose is to find out where the large and decisive mass of swing voters is located. But most important, polls tell what issues the voters really care about and how deeply they care.

The *American Institute of Public Opinion*, better known as the *Gallup Poll*, was established for the purpose of sounding the public's views on the important political, social, and economic issues of the day.

This was to be a new and exciting venture in journalism, producing news of a different type. The press, and the press services, confine their efforts almost entirely to reporting events—to what people *do*. This new effort was to deal with a new aspect of life—what people *think*. A new dimension to the news was to be added. In the words of a famous editor and publisher, Roy Howard, a "Fifth Estate" was born with modern polling.

One of the most important contributions which sample surveys of the population, or segments of the population, can offer is in the improvement of government. The modern poll can, and to a certain extent does, function as the *creative arm of government*. It can discover the likely response of the public to any new proposal, law, or innovation. It can do this by presenting ideas to the public for their appraisal and judgment—ideas that range all the way from specific proposals for dealing with strikes and racial problems to proposals for ending the war in Vietnam.

Let us look briefly at some proposals and what the public has to say about them.

A majority of Americans would like to overhaul the whole process of electing a president—they favor nationwide primaries; making the conventions, if held, more dignified; shortening the campaign; abandoning the present electoral college system. Our fellow citizens would also like to see the voting age lowered to 18.

Americans favor stiffer laws on drinking and driving; tougher gun laws; less leniency toward criminals on the part of courts; compulsory arbitration in the case of strikes, particularly those strikes

affecting the public welfare; tougher laws on por-
nography; guaranteed work rather than a guaranteed annual income—arising out of the conviction
that people ought to be helped, but ought not to get
"something for nothing."

Americans think all young men should be re-
quired to give one year's service to their country—
either in the armed forces or in some non-military
work, such as VISTA or the Peace Corps.

The list could be expanded greatly. The fact of
the matter is, America would be a far different place
in which to live if many of the public's long-sought
reforms were translated into law—and, I think, a
better place.

The desire for change on the part of the public
is not something new—we have found it for years. If
you sense a bias in my remarks—a bias in favor of
the average citizen—you are probably right. From
years of seeing how the average citizen reacts to
ideas of a great range, it is not difficult to believe
that his thinking is sound, his common sense quo-
tient high. Congressional action, as a matter of fact,
supports this belief. Sooner or later the public's will
is translated into law.

More and more the modern poll is dealing with
new ideas—proposals for dealing in new ways with
current problems.

The poll in this respect has a natural advantage over legislators. It can go directly to the people without fear of political repercussions. It can determine the degree of acceptance or resistance to any proposal—its appeal or lack of appeal, at least in its early stages of acceptance or rejection. It is this creative function that may, in the years ahead, offer the public opinion poll its greatest opportunity for service to the nation.

CHAPTER NINE

Television
Distortion
in Political
Reporting

by

Kurt Lang

Professor of Sociology, State University of New York

and

Gladys Engel Lang

Senior Research Associate,
Bureau of Applied Social Research, Columbia University

PROFESSORS KURT AND GLADYS LANG began the study of television's peculiar political effects at a time when that medium was just becoming a mass communication vehicle in the true sense of the word. They have continued work in this area and have produced, in the past year, a book entitled *Politics and Television* that gathers together some of their studies of the past 20 years. The Langs are also the authors of *Collective Dynamics*.

Professor Gladys Engel Lang received degrees from the University of Michigan and from the University of Washington. She was an information analyst for the Office of War Information, then worked for the Office of Strategic Services until 1949. In 1950, she and Professor Lang were married, and she returned to school, taking a doctorate in sociology at the University of Chicago in 1954.

Since 1954, she has been associated with Carleton (Ottawa), College, Brooklyn College, Queens College, Washington University in St. Louis, Rutgers, and the graduate journalism program at Columbia University. In 1965 she became a senior research sociologist at the Center of Urban Education and became assistant director of that organization. She is now senior research associate of the Bureau of Applied Social Research at Columbia University and a lecturer on the graduate faculty of the Department of Sociology.

Professor Kurt Lang was born in Berlin and served in the U. S. Army during World War II. After the war he worked in the government's denazification program of Germany, and as a research analyst on political affairs, then as research associate for the committee on communications at the University of Chicago. He was graduated from Chicago in 1949 and took masters and doctoral degrees from the same school in 1952 and 1953.

He was research sociologist for the Canadian Broadcasting Corporation for several years in the mid-1950's, and has been a member of the faculties of the University of Miami, Queens College, University of California (Berkeley), and most recently, professor of sociology at the State University of New York at Stony Brook.

TELEVISION HAS EXTENDED the visual dimensions of the area of public life. Yet events, as we see them on video, never present a faithful mirror of reality. TV is more like a prism than a mirror. The light rays of events are bent as they pass through, so that the picture of public life conveyed over television is a refracted image. This is one central theme of our book, *Television and Politics,** which reports studies we made of major political spectacles televised over the years since TV became a mass medium.

The first study in that book was of General MacArthur's triumphal return to America in 1951. The critical comment of one influential book reviewer makes us acutely aware that much time has passed since. "What," he asked, "is new about the discovery that TV journalism often falls short of the 'truth' in its revelations or that, in other words, a picture is not always worth a thousand words—or even a hundred?" The two of us recall vividly how often during the 1950's TV-journalists hid behind that cliche, rejecting, sometimes with indignation, any evidence—even that based on systematic observation and analysis—that an event like MacArthur Day in Chicago was a rather different experience for those on the streets and those in the TV audience. In the words of one network news execu-

* Quadrangle Books, 1968.

tive, all we can do with our cameras is to lay things before people while they are happening the way they are happening; if they don't understand what's going on, that is their fault—not the fault of the medium.

Yet this reviewer has a point. Today TV journalists are far more introspective and sophisticated about their work than they were a decade ago. Many of the new generation have never worked in any other medium, whereas the pioneer group, largely recruited from radio, was especially impressed with the actuality they could create by adding the visual dimension. Meanwhile an entirely new audience has also come of age. Young people nowadays take television for granted; they never knew a world without TV and appear to be less awed and more skeptical about the use to which the medium is put.

In addition, some recent events have contributed to this skepticism. First, the news media generally, and television in particular, have been publicly criticized for the allegedly irresponsible coverage they gave to radical black power advocates and leaders of the student left. The overdose of attention given these individuals, it was said, inflated their importance. It left the impression that their actual following was far larger than it was and that their words carried more weight than they really did. TV, it was charged, did more than merely report their activities; it helped build them up. If this was one criticism, the Kerner Commission emphasized another: the news media—including TV— in their day-to-day reporting of news from the ghetto neglected positive developments toward self-help, community organization, and the creative achievement of Negroes in various fields in favor of news about crime, addiction, ignorance, and other pathological manifestations. More specifically, the Kerner Commission, while giving good marks to TV for its riot coverage, pointed out that on several occasions reporters had staged violence explicitly for the benefit of the cameras. Similar lapses also came to light during the violence surrounding the Democratic convention. At that time also, the network news departments were accused of deliberately dramatizing police brutality against demonstrators without giving adequate play to the provocations leading to what the Walker Report called a "police riot."

These relatively recent attacks on the objectivity of TV raise questions about unbalanced reporting, semi-fakery, and even of deliberate one-sided distortion. Important as these questions are, our interest today is in something else—in the more subtle and yet more pervasive sources of distortion, in the conceptions and points of view that inevitably enter into the unique perspective from which television views an event. We begin by noting that it is obviously as impossible to cover a complex event from every angle as it is for a participant to be everywhere at the same time. Thus, the objectivity of a television report, like the objectivity of all reporting, depends on judgments rather than the abeyance of judgment. These judgments give political events a structure they may not actually have. Note how often the viewer is reminded during a live telecast that he sees *more clearly* and *knows more* about what is going on than people at the scene. This is even recognized by politicians who monitor the news. The reporter who uses a televised statement by one politician to elicit a televised response from another politician is in fact initiating a dialogue and imposing a structure where none existed before.

Political news that reaches the public through live telecasts or in regularly scheduled TV news programs is the product of internal decisions. As in other news media, selectivity is inevitably involved. Only some events end up as news and the number singled out for live coverage is even smaller. Yet there are considerations in television coverage that have little or no relevance to decisions in other media.

The first concerns the deployment of cameras and equipment in locations suitable for visual coverage. Cameras are obviously less mobile than the roving eyes of reporters and so many decisions need to be made in advance. This is true both in preparing a regular program and in live telecasts of special events. In both cases the coverage is influenced by ideas about how the equipment can be put to best use.

A second set of considerations concerns the extent to which news content is, or should be, guided by available visual material and commentary restricted to what is shown on the screen. Whatever the decision, it affects the image the viewer perceives, particularly when events shown are ambiguous.

There is a third set of considerations that relates to reciprocal effects. Newsmen claim that they merely report the news and that they do this to the best of their ability, but there is clear evidence that television by its presence transforms certain events in ways that other news media do not. For example, demonstrators who raise their voices and perhaps even their fists as the cameras approach may appear to be frenzied members of a crowd unaware of the consequences of their actions. Although such "spontaneous" events are often addressed directly to the camera, it is difficult for the TV crew to turn away. Not only is the demonstration itself "newsworthy" but if turn away they did, they would immediately open themselves to a charge of suppression and, whether guilty or not, magnify the event even more. Newsmen are very much aware that some political "events" are deliberately stage-managed for the TV audience, as at party conventions that have been redesigned to give aspiring young politicians free air time and to project an image of party unity, leaving the more significant battles to be fought out in advance or in the wings. Television thus becomes fond of taking the viewer backstage in search of the real show. This looking for the action wherever it is may help to keep the political establishment honest but sometimes it causes an uproar, as when a reporter exceeds his role and intrudes himself into the proceedings. Similarly, when a network looking for interesting interludes builds up excitement about a contest already resolved or about one that never really existed, it may not be deliberately slanting the news but it can affect the shape of events. The Kennedy boomlet at the last convention became a real political factor as TV talked it up. This made it impossible for the press in writing about the day's developments to ignore.

Fourth, there are TV-*created* events, even though they can never be manufactured out of whole cloth. In some instances the event happens only because of television—as when we are dealing with an interview show, televised debates, or the fast count and projection of early election returns when the major news services pool their resources. In other instances, television itself becomes the "event." Thus, it is quite clear by hindsight that the furore in 1952 over whether TV should cover the platform and credentials hearings provided the Eisenhower forces with an issue that helped assure his victory over Taft. They clearly exploited the presence of television to transform a simple procedural issue into an issue of "fair play"—a moral issue. Elmer Davis said at the time this proved it was no longer possible to commit grand larceny in broad daylight. On the contrary, it demonstrated an effective political exploitation of television by the Eisenhower forces.

Whether created by TV or not, televised political events are bona fide news stories for the print media. The talk of the town and the write-up in the press often follow the televised version. As for the viewing public, despite some loss of naivete, most remain convinced that they can see for themselves. They are confident—as the flood of letters about Chicago indicated—that they cannot be fooled, that they can spot any bias. News, once defined as that which is published, becomes increasingly—for millions of Americans—that which is televised. There are people for whom television is the sole political reality—the only medium through which they keep themselves informed. These people—speaking with Will Rogers—know only what they see on their television screens. The political significance of the distortions inherent in TV reporting hinges to a large degree on the confidence people have in the televised image and on their reliance on it.

There is indeed a fascination about the way television brings events into focus and that sense of fascination, though jaded, has by no means been lost. It is, moreover, to some extent shared by nearly all people. Yet McLuhan, when he contends that television tunes the viewer into what is happening as if he were a participant in the global village, seems to confuse the sense of participation with the content that this experience provides. Electronic participation is clearly different from actual participation and TV news, by bringing the world closer, only forces us to live a larger part of our lives at a distance. The McLuhanite metaphor is true only insofar as a televised event provokes a mass reaction, a reaction that can extend to the entire world.

But as soon as we move beyond metaphor to

get down to details, it becomes all too clear that there is a great deal about media use that we don't now understand but need to understand if we are to understand the role of television in political life. For one thing, TV news directors know relatively little about their audiences, though such knowledge is probably more important to them than to the typical newspaper editor because, unlike the latter whose paper rarely has a significant circulation outside the local community, network news broadcasts are geared to a nationwide audience. Yet we have only the vaguest idea about how those who follow the news via Huntley-Brinkley may differ from the Cronkite crowd. Both staffs know they have a mass audience made up of people with widely diverse backgrounds and motivations. It is clearly not possible to adapt the content of news to the needs, knowledge, and interests of particular types of viewers if practically nothing beyond ratings and a few elementary ideas about the sex, age, educational level, and so forth is known of one's audience. The problem is less acute for the newspaper because the paper as a whole is a conglomerate from among which people select what they want.

Nevertheless, the TV journalist, like his newspaper colleague, bases his operations on some image of his audience. What characteristics do they keep in mind? Some have charged that the TV newsman goes the mass entertainment route, seeking to satisfy the greatest number of potential customers while dissatisfying the fewest. John Hohenberg of Columbia's Graduate School of Journalism evidently thinks TV has so catered to a mass audience. Broadcast journalism, he says, gears its news coverage to the lowest level of intelligence represented in its audience.

Whatever target audience news personnel do have in mind, we are inclined to dispute this allegation. For, the audience whose approval the electronic journalists seek consists, as it does everywhere, largely of their professional colleagues, including technical crews whose reactions they feel are closer to the gut feelings of the average man. We also believe that the way political news is handled on the usual news show makes it pretty confusing to many viewers whose intelligence isn't at the lowest level. To understand it calls for a good deal of prior knowledge that many viewers lack. The crisp bulletins in which complicated developments are reported on the ordinary news show, the filmed interview that elicits the quotable statement without context or evaluation, the shift from one scene or one crisis to the next, and so forth, are often difficult to grasp. It is to this fragmentation of news into headlines, to the emphasis on the unusual and extraordinary, on crises and conflict, at the expense of depth that Hohenberg really directs his objection. These deficiencies are real; they have no doubt increased as news shows have attracted more advertisers and begun to pay off. The amount of hard news declined, making way for gimmicks leading into commercials that had already cut into the time available for news. Television news, as it exists, obviously falls far short of meeting the minimal information requirements of the public.

A number one issue is whether the coverage of news on TV is now, or can be in the immediate future, tailored to two different groups that comprise the mass audience in which television takes justified pride. There is, first, the print-oriented group who use TV news as a supplement to reading newspapers and news magazines. Many people obviously like to see on their screen the events and the people they read about. They deliberately seek out the news for its content. The other part of the audience is electronic-oriented. Its members are heavy TV-users, mostly of the entertainment fare. For its news it relies exclusively on broadcast journalism—usually on TV in the evening and radio in the morning. The TV news serves different functions for the two groups and like exposure must result in quite different impressions. The electronically-oriented group deserves special emphasis in any discussion of TV distortion; their political world is in large measure an electronic creation.

Some recent surveys, some still under way, point to the urban poor as among those most dependent on television for knowledge of what is happening. Thus, a significant minority of urban blacks do not read news but listen with reasonable regularity in the morning to news on the radio and watch the TV news in the evening. The fact that the great majority of these poor black families have more than one TV set in working order testifies to the significant part that TV plays in their lives. Though they are an important part of the audience for news, we know less than we should about the picture of the world these people get from television. Undereducated as they may be, these people, like others, are hungry for knowledge, and value the familiarity with objects, events, and personalities outside their immediate experience.

For the resident of the black slum, television is a medium controlled by the establishment. When people like himself appear on the news, it is usually because they have either got into some kind of trouble or forced the establishment to take note.

Most of what such a person knows about his own community he finds out as he walks down the street. Since the Kerner Report, television news has been paying more attention to the ghetto, and the more TV covers the ghetto, the easier it will be for the black viewer to judge how authentically TV handles the news. Nevertheless, most of what anyone sees on television still concerns distant events where it is not possible to validate impressions against one's own experience. There is no evidence so far that any distrust of TV, whether for its neglect or mis-handling of ghetto news, affects the credibility of TV in its handling of events outside the ghetto. In either case, the viewer "sees for himself;" he feels his conclusions have a basis in experience.

There is, moreover, a paradox in TV's being, at one and the same time, a mass medium and an es-tablishment medium. This transforms it into a medium of confrontation. People become agitated over issues with which they have little familiarity and react to them as if they really knew. Is there anyone among us who has not recently found himself in a discussion about student protest—by blacks or whites—with someone who has seldom, if ever, set foot on a college campus and who, it would seem, had little stake or interest in decisions about curriculum—yet was terribly worked up about doing something to put an end to all this protest by calling the cops to bash some heads and throw the recalcitrants in jail? Try telling these people how complicated some of the issues are. Many will tell you they *know;* they have, after all, been watching it on TV! Those of us trying to follow events on our campus do not always have a clear idea of what is going on, while many a TV viewer feels that he does.

In concluding this talk, we would like to raise three related questions about the coverage of politics by television: first, whether television is really suited to—or should be—handling every kind of news; second, whether the relationship between the printed news media and electronic news media should be changed, and whether it can; and, third, what is the appropriate division of labor within television for the best overall coverage of the news?

Whether or not TV can and really should broadcast every kind of news has to the best of our knowledge never been raised—and raising it is sure to arouse the wrath of TV journalists who have fought so hard to be included wherever other journalists are. We are not challenging the effectiveness of television as measured by the audiences it commands or as a medium through which information of every kind, including spot news, can be quickly disseminated. Here television has taken over much of the role radio carved out for itself in the 1930's when people first turned to their sets to keep abreast with the developing war crisis. Yet television has blazed few new trails in this area. The unique contribution of television has been in the opportunity it affords for certain live broadcasts of major public events.

What television does best is to cover events that are scheduled and to which men and resources can be dispatched in advance. Thus, television does best in handling pageants, parades, political and athletic contests, parliamentary debates, inaugurations. On the other hand, it seems impossible to report live, or even visually to recapture, with any real authenticity such complex and fast-moving events as the continuing battles in Vietnam or those on the streets of Detroit in 1967 or in Chicago in 1968. Arguments about coverage usually revolve around whether the elements are being presented in the proper balance—for example, is too much attention given to the crowds in the streets? Are there too many pictures of the actual fighting? Our own view is that the appropriate coverage in depth can only be achieved by a carefully edited documentary—a form of presentation at which the networks at times have truly excelled. Obviously the issue is not the right to cover or the amount of coverage but the kind of coverage. In Chicago, for example, both TV cameras and reporters dutifully covered the presence of thousands of young people and their subsequent clashes with local police and National Guardsmen. Here, it would seem, was a marvelous opportunity for an exploration in depth, as part of the live convention coverage, about what the demonstrations by so many young and some older people really meant. Why should so many of them be walking around with Vietcong flags and shouting, "We want to destroy this whole rotten society and bring the establishment tumbling down?" In covering the violence as it was happening, the networks did manage to catch a good deal of the drama without being able to convey thereby what Chicago presaged for both the Democratic party and the growth of the radical movement.

Our point is that the TV documentary—a meticulously edited version of some events, which actually may no longer be news—is often journalistically more desirable than on-the-spot reporting. It may lack actuality, which is the unique asset of TV, but it may result in better TV reporting, though at the risk that editorial judgments intrude themselves.

Our second question has to do with the relation between the printed news media and television. It is generally taken for granted that the broadcasters can get out the news faster and will therefore take over on-the-spot reporting. Though newspapers sometimes report a major newsbreak that received full video coverage as if only reporters but not their readers had watched it on TV, there is at least a grudging awareness that they must adapt themselves to the medium they consider an arch rival. In television no similar problem seems to be recognized. The journalists here tend to respond to criticism by pointing to limitations of time and resources, which it is up to the newspaper to supplement. Yet insofar as television does manage to alert and to arouse people, should it not also direct its viewers to sources of information from which the background necessary for full understanding can be secured?

The roles of the various news media in relation to one another are constantly undergoing change. There is, for example, a very real prospect that in the not-too-distant future we will distribute newspaper "copies" electronically over TV. The distinction between the two media would thus be blurred. Each channel would then have an option between formats in which to transmit the news—as electronic newspapers, in the form of radio-type bulletins, in film clips, in mixtures, or as carefully constructed documentaries.

Finally, there is the question of the division of labor within television itself. Many local news shows recall radio; their pictorial content is minimal and often confined to visual vignettes of rather trivial events. Would it not be better for most television stations to confine themselves to brief periodic news broadcasts—perhaps even without any visual content—while other stations might take on the job of full reporting of the news in depth? As in radio now, we could have all-news stations in which major documentaries alternated with taped interviews and news reported, insofar as possible, on film. The special local coverage given by some community stations is an alternative that already exists. New cable systems will open more channels so that we will soon be able to match the diversity we now have on radio.

Other technological innovations now on the horizon open still other possibilities. Satellites are bringing in live pictures from many parts of the world and before too long some of the selection now under the control of the news director will pass into the hands of the viewer. He will be able to decide among several transmissions going on concurrently, and with video-tape recorders for home use now on the market and with programs soon to be marketed the capacity to supply information into the TV-oriented home increases greatly.

So far as news possibilities are concerned, the problem will be one of saturation rather than paucity. Some preselection by editors will still be needed to guide viewers. In political communication, as elsewhere, there is a division of labor. Even if the main tool of the political analyst is the camera, he continues to assume the expert role in political communication. We can never be certain of his sense of social responsibility. But of one thing we can be sure: that the system of political communication, regardless of its technological base, remains essentially a human system subject to errors of judgment, of deliberate bias, and attempts at manipulation. The visual dimension cannot eliminate the human dimension, and we ought to be aware that things, even on television, are not always quite what they seem.

CHAPTER TEN

Politics and the Press: A Final Comment

by

Irving Dilliard

Ferris Professor of Journalism, Princeton University

PROFESSOR IRVING DILLIARD was an editorial writer for the *St. Louis Post-Dispatch* for thirty years—years in which the *Post-Dispatch* gained a reputation as one of this country's, as well as the world's, best newspapers. For nine of those years he was editor of the editorial page. Professor Dilliard has been a life-long student and observer of—as well as a participant in—journalism, government, and education.

In journalism, he has held the office of national president of Sigma Delta Chi, journalism's professional society. He was in the first class of Nieman Fellows; and he has been selected as a Fellow in Sigma Delta Chi. He is at present the Ferris Professor of Journalism at Princeton University.

In government he has long been an observer of the Supreme Court and has written or edited *Mr. Justice Brandeis, Great American; The Spirit of Liberty: Papers and Addresses of Learned Hand;* and *One Man's Stand for Freedom: Mr. Justice Black and the Bill of Rights.* And, he is known nationally for his work in the area of civil liberties.

In education, he served as a member of the board of trustees at the University of Illinois from 1961 to 1967. He was graduated from the University of Illinois, and six honorary doctorates have been conferred upon him.

I CONSIDER OUR PRESS the best and the freest in the world. I don't know of any that is better anywhere. But it is not above improvement and it certainly is worth saving. I am delighted to know that so many fine young Americans are training themselves for different aspects of it.

Let me tell you quickly the names of four editors that I think of as outstanding practitioners of our craft. They happen to be on relatively small papers. One is in the North, one is in the East, one is in the West, and one is in the South. N-E-W-S, news, so to speak.

Oddly enough, each one is a man of greatly advanced years. If I looked around for the young editors, I am not sure I would find many who are as vigorous in their minds as these have been.

Josiah William Gitt publishes the *York* (Pennsylvania) *Gazette and Daily*. He didn't have to wait until things began to go badly in Vietnam to decide that the war was an immoral war and we shouldn't be in it. This was his attitude right from the beginning.

When he became convinced, ahead of the Surgeon-General's report, that the *Gazette and Daily* should no longer be pushing cigarettes on its readers through advertising, he notified the agency, "no more cigarette advertising in the *Gazette and*

Daily," and stopped further contracts, just like that.

In the North, I would pick William Theodore Evjue of the *Madison* (Wisconsin) *Capital Times*. In 1917, when the editor of a Madison newspaper denounced Senator LaFollette as a treasonable, traitorous person in effect, Mr. Evjue, who was business manager, walked into the publisher's office and resigned. Within a few days, almost hours, he started the *Capital Times.*

He survived boycotts and everything else. In the 1950's his was just about the first paper in the country to undress Senator Joe McCarthy.

He, like Mr. Gitt, is well beyond the age of eighty today.

In the South I'd name John Netherland Heiskell of the *Arkansas Gazette*. Because of its policies, his paper saw its circulation go down and its advertising dwindle at the time of the Little Rock troubles over public school desegregation.

Mr. Heiskell is more than ninety.

My fourth would be Thomas More Storke of the *Santa Barbara* (California) *News-Press*. If any paper told what the John Birch Society was like ahead of Mr. Storke's, I don't know what paper it was.

I mention these four to show that this sort of

outstanding public service happens today in newspapers. But they don't have to be the major papers in the country in terms of size, circulation, and reputation.

The story about Justice Fortas is a major accomplishment that I would much rather have seen in the newspaper than in *Life* magazine. I don't object to its being in *Life*—indeed, I'm glad to see *Life* picking up the muckraking tradition of sixty years ago. There hasn't been enough of it, in either the magazines or the newspapers, in the sense of disclosure of the things we need to know. This was quite a beat, and *Life* developed the facts so that all the newspapers of the country had to take notice. In the end, a Supreme Court justice had to resign, and for the first time in history, leave under pressure of public criticism.

Of course, this makes it most fortunate that Mr. Fortas was not promoted to chief justice last year because it would have been more embarrassing for the chief justice to have to go through what he has just gone through.

It suggests to young people, it seems to me, that there are other things in life than money and monetary rewards. Whatever you do, don't make money your basic criterion.

We need a press that is much more alert in the

future to many urgent matters. I don't know how you feel about the Vietnam war. It seems to me it has been pretty well disowned by the press today as well as by people over the country. This does not mean that there are not still some who are attached to it as a cause we ought to stand by. I don't mean to argue it one way or the other. But, if the press feels this way about it now, where was the press in the days when this war could have been headed off?

Back in 1954, before Dien Bien Phu fell, a certain editorial writer heard Mr. Nixon, then vice president, address the American Society of Newspaper Editors and say that it might very well be necessary to put American troops in Indochina to save the French. And at almost that same moment, on April 26 of that year, President Eisenhower was ready to go before Congress and ask for an American strike at Dien Bien Phu. The British wouldn't go along and we didn't make that strike.

But this editorial writer, on hearing Mr. Nixon say that we might very well put ground troops in there to shore up the French, went back to his newspaper and wrote an editorial entitled, "A War to Stay Out Of."

This was May 5, 1954, and the editorial concluded, "This paper does not question President Eisenhower's ability as a military leader or his experience in world affairs. On the contrary, we readily recognize these as primary among the qualities for which he was so overwhelmingly elected the nation's chief executive. But Dwight D. Eisenhower, like every president before him, needs the benefit of public opinion to help him in the wise conduct of his heavily-burdened office.

"To that constructive end we state that it is our profound conviction that the Indo-Chinese War is a war to stay out of. Let Washington take no more steps that may have the effect of edging us closer to military engagement in Indo-China. Let our government end our war-like acts that can now be charged against us by the Indo-Chinese rebels"— because it was a civil war. They were fighting against the colonial power that they wanted to throw out.

"Let there be no more hasty, irresponsible statements about Indo-China by our public officials. Let us, instead, with our allies, in the President's own words, (quoting Eisenhower) do what we can to 'Work out a practical way of getting along in the world.'"

That is what we are going to have to do now, fifteen years later and 35,000 young Americans later. After Dien Bien Phu fell, there was an editorial entitled, "War to Stay Out Of II"—the paper had three of them, because after Dien Bien Phu fell, there was a big agitation to take over the whole lost cause.

Newspapers need to look ahead in the matters of our political life. It seems to me that it was absolutely clear that Johnson wouldn't run again. And yet this came as a great surprise to the country. On February 28, 1968, the *Wall Street Journal* had a story, "The War President"—Johnson now stresses Vietnam military effort, instead of peace talks; more troops, money likely; new case for a tax increase, and so on. Johnson's only interest then, apparently, was to prosecute the war. And yet, on March 31, hardly a month later, Johnson withdrew.

And this, it seems to me, was clear as daylight—that you could figure out why he wouldn't run again. I'd like to see the press do its home work more than it has done in the past.

Here is why it was clear that Johnson wouldn't run again. The year 1942 was the only year like 1966 in our recent history. Roosevelt had been overwhelmingly reelected in 1940, and 1942 was the first congressional election after that. But in the off-year in between, 1941, came Pearl Harbor.

If any president should have been sustained, it was Roosevelt in 1942. He should have been sustained by the voters that year because the Japanese bombed us at Pearl Harbor and Hitler declared war on us from the other side. That was very different from 1966 when we were in a war a lot of people, rightly or wrongly, think we went around the world to start for no good reason.

What happened in 1942? Plenty. We were until late Wednesday after the election that year finding out whether or not the Republicans had won enough seats to take over the speakership. That would have been a terrific repudiation of FDR and the war effort. But this was all clear, too. So clear that I wrote an article for the *New Republic* that ran in September called, "Can the Republicans Win?" And it spelled out all the attitudes that would cause the American people to vote against the Democrats in favor of the Republicans. The Gallup Poll was wrong that year.

I talked with Eric Goldman, who wrote the book, *The Tragedy of Lyndon Johnson,* when I saw him at Princeton in the spring of 1966. He was on the White House staff then.

I asked how things were going in Washington.

He said, "We can't get Johnson's interest in anything except the war."

And I said, "But hadn't he better pay some attention to congressional elections?"

He asked, "Why is that?"

And I said, "Well, the Democrats are going to take a bad beating in November."

"Oh," Goldman said, "Johnson has a Gallup Poll here and a Harris Poll there and the Roper Poll in still another pocket. All these polls are sustaining him."

I said, "Well, you tell him how wrong the Gallup Poll was in 1942 and maybe it might make a difference."

So, Goldman went back to Washington, got out the *New Republic* article, and circulated it in the White House. He wrote me and said, in effect, "Watch things begin to happen."

The first thing that happened was that the President appointed a big commission to overhaul the draft because that was one of the chief causes for dissatisfaction.

But the point is that by midsummer, the Democrats around Johnson knew that they were going to lose many seats in November.

Senator Paul Douglas from Illinois had gone to the White House and said, "I'll be defeated unless I have some outstanding help." What he meant was that Johnson was going to have to go into Illinois and speak for him and say, "I need Paul Douglas, who's been right on the Great Society and who has held up my hands on the Vietnam war." Because Douglas had. Douglas, a Marine veteran, had supported Johnson on the war when a lot of people had not.

What did Johnson do? In my judgment, he simply ran out on all the people who put through the Great Society. And that is why I think he timed the trip to the Manila Conference so he wouldn't have to be at home in October taking part in the campaign.

The upshot of this was that he did not campaign. He let down the whole group which got the Great Society legislation through. He announced, when he got back to Washington, that he was going to the hospital and have an operation. He took almost no part in the campaign. And many who put through the Great Society went down in defeat. They lost around 45 House seats and Senate seats and a large number of governorships. Of course that set the stage for what happened two years later.

I would like to see more attention paid by the press to the points that explain events. This is one of the relationships that I suggest be developed much more closely with respect to our newspapers and our politics.

As an example, let us consider an aspect of the Riot Commission that was created in 1967 by Lyndon B. Johnson through issuance of an executive order. This is the commission to whose chairmanship the President appointed then Gov. Kerner of Illinois. As a consequence Gov. Kerner's name was so widely associated with this important White House commission that its report has come to be known popularly as "the Kerner Commission Report."

No one has told me what I am about to say. It is my own speculation entirely. Not a one of you needs to believe it or indeed any part of it. I happen to think that it makes sense and if it does to you as well, it may then illustrate my proposal that the press pay more attention to the points that explain events.

Because of the extreme importance of the work of the Riot Commission—its official name was the National Advisory Commission on Civil Disorders—President Johnson and his staff advisers undoubtedly decided that the Chairman should be a Democrat. If the Chairman was to be a Democrat, then the Vice Chairman would need to be a Republican. The choice of the Republican for Vice Chairman was so obvious that there could hardly be any other one considered. He was of course the Mayor of the country's largest city, John V. Lindsay of New York. This selection seems to me to be so plain that it does not require any supporting argument or evidence.

So far so good. With Republican Mayor Lindsay, because of his party and his post, a sure choice for the Vice Chairmanship, the White House had its work cut out for it. Namely, to find a Democrat who would outrank the Vice Chairman. That meant a Democratic Governor.

Let's look at a map of the United States as the presidential staff goes about picking its Democratic Governor. For he cannot be just any Democratic Governor. He cannot be the Democratic Governor of some rural Southern State. He cannot be the Democratic Governor of some thinly populated Western State. He must be the Democratic Governor of a Northern State who has had some first-hand experience with civil disorders and riots.

Again so far so good. With these qualifications in mind we begin looking for our Democratic Governor. We start at the right hand side of the map with Massachusetts, the Democratic State of the Democratic Kennedys. Massachusetts not only has the Boston regional complex but is highly urbanized generally. But we do not tarry long in Massachusetts since its Governor, Volpe, is a Republican. We proceed West and cross into New York. Here the Governor is Rockefeller, another Republican, so we keep on going. We drop down into Pennsylvania and find another Republican Governor and when we move on West into Ohio it is more of the same. Indeed, we go all the way to California and find that the one major State with a large urban population and a vast metropolitan complex that also has a Democratic Governor is Illinois.

Someone says: You are overlooking New Jersey which has a Democratic Governor. No, we are not. But New Jersey is even more of an Atlantic Coast State than is New York and the Chairman and Vice Chairman cannot come from what is in effect the same metropolitan area. Nor do we overlook Missouri, for example. Our need is for a Democratic Governor from a State with 10,000,000 or more people and so it has to be Illinois and that State's Governor is Otto Kerner.

That in short is why I think Kerner was appointed chairman of the Riot Commission. If anyone else has a better explanation I would like to hear of it. The very next year, while Kerner was still Governor, the assassination of the Rev. Martin Luther King, Jr., touched off rioting and burning in Washington and certain other major cities. One of them was Chicago where block after block was set afire. My recollection is that Governor Kerner was on vacation at the time and it was the Lieutenant

Governor, Samuel Shapiro, who had to cope with the disorders and violence in the nation's second largest city.

The most important part of this Commission's report from the standpoint of the press, in my judgment, was not highlighted by the press so far as I know. I refer particularly to the first sentence of a newsbearing paragraph on page 384 of the Commission's printed report (Bantam Books edition). It read: "The journalistic profession has been shockingly backward in seeking out, hiring, training and promoting Negroes."

To me that was the big news in the report from the standpoint of the press. Nothing the report said about other aspects of the racial problem or about race and crime compared with this indictment of the newspapers themselves. Yet how many newspapers carried editorials discussing this indictment or even denying it? How many printed, as they should have done, this sentence in bold-faced type? How many printed it at all?

There were some newspapers that did print this news and I am sure that a few even commented on it. But I know the press well enough to say that there were precious few. I do not hesitate to say that in many, many newspapers—perhaps the vast majority—this news did not appear at all. The editors and publishers of these papers did not use any of their space telling their readers that, in the opinion of the President's Commission on Civil Disorders, "the journalistic profession has been shockingly backward in seeking out, hiring, training and promoting Negroes." I repeat this indictment deliberately.

From personal experience I know how the newspaper world avoided facing up to the matter of employing from racial minorities. Some 20 or more years ago, I proposed at the *St. Louis Post-Dispatch* that one or two Negro office boys be engaged as a means of starting promising young members of the race up the ladder of employment in the various departments, news, commercial, business, advertising and so on. I was not only willing but eager to have this begin in the editorial page department in the hope that we could give some Negro youths an incentive to complete their education and prepare themselves for careers in journalism. I remember only too well what a high-ranking member of the administrative organization of the *Post-Dispatch* said about "the problems" that employment of Negroes would raise. I called his attention to the fact that employing Negroes as cleaners and custodians did not produce problems. Why, I asked, should a Negro office boy be more of a problem than a Negro janitor? If that was the administrative guidance at the *Post-Dispatch* at that time, there can be little question as to what it was on newspapers generally.

Let me turn back to our beginning. We do have the best and the freest press in the world. But this is not to boast. So much improvement is in order. The record of the press is not only too little and too late, but it is too little and too late far too often. It needs to catch up, gain the initiative and keep ahead.

That is the way to make the daily job of getting out a newspaper fascinating, challenging, absorbing. It is the way to make our work captivating, rewarding, fulfilling. There are no time servers, no clock watchers, where everyone has a part to play in the continuous public service that only a newspaper can provide.

Index

A

Anti-Ballistic Missile System 67, 100
Adversary relationship of press & politician 9-10, 52, 56, 63, 73
African Methodist Episcopal Church 40-41
Agnew, Spiro T. 7-8, 10, 112
Aslop, Stewart 54-55
American Society of Newspaper Editors 175
Appraising press coverage of politics 35-55
Arkansas Gazette 173
Associated Press 56
Attlee, Clement 26

B

Baltimore Sun 9-10, 48, 62, 111-115
Bias, see News
Bill of Rights 108
Blacks: Blacks & the Press 117-128; Black militants 124, 150-157; Black press 126-128; Black reporters 121, 123, 127-28, 184-186
Boston Globe 115
Boston, Massachusetts 43
Bowles, Chester 42
Brinkley, David 62, 80, 157

Britain 9, 20, 23-24, 27-29, 97, 175
Broder, David S. 9-10, 57-74, 114-115; biography 59
Brown, George 26
Brown, Rap 124
Buffalo, New York 65-66
Bunche, Ralph 41

C

California primary (1968) 132
Cantrill, Hadley 139
Carmichael, Stokely 124
Carter, Richard 39
Cater, Douglass 108
Chandler, Otis 10, 75-88; biography 77-78
Chicago Democratic Convention (1968) 113, 115, 151, 155, 163-164; Demonstrations 81, 86-87, 122
Christian Anti-Communism Crusade 44-46
Christian, George 94
Christian Science Monitor 114
Civil rights 42, 101
Cleveland, Ohio 66
Community Antenna Television 166
Congress 66-68, 99, 108, 177-180

Conrad, Paul 84
Conservative Party (Britain) 28
Constitution 49
Constitutional Convention 49-50
Cornwell, Elmer E., Jr. 9, 13-33;
    biography 15
Credibility 48, 61, 75-88, 80, 102;
    credibility gap 7, 10, 30, 32, 56,
    60, 79, 82-85 15-86
Cronkite, Walter 62, 157

D

Daley, Richard 81, 86
Davis, Elmer 155
Day, Robin 27
DeGaulle, Charles 21
Democratic party 39, 41, 54, 69-
    70, 86, 98-99, 109, 164, 178,
    182; Reform Committee 69-70;
    Chicago Convention—see
    Chicago
Department of Agriculture 96
Department of Health, Education,
    and Welfare 96
Department of Housing and Ur-
    ban Development 96
De Moines, Iowa 8
Detroit, Michigan 163
Dewey, Thomas 139-140
Dien Bien Phu 175-77
Dilliard, Irving 11, 169-186;
    biography 171
Disraeli, Benjamin 30, 108
Douglas, Paul 179-80
Douglas-Home, Sir Alex 27
Durant, Henry 134

E

Eden, Anthony 25
Editorials, newspaper 98-100
Eisenhower, Dwight D. 31-32,
    155, 175-76; Administration 53
Emancipation Proclamation 53

Evans, Sir Harold 24
Evjue, William Theodore 173

F

Federal budget 66
Fortas, Abe 174
France 175
Furguson, Ernest B. 112

G

Gaitskell, Hugh 26
Gallup, George Jr. 11, 129-143,
    133-134; biography 131
Gallup, George Sr. 136-137, 139
Gallup Poll 29, 32, 132-43, 178
Georgia, University of 8
Ghetto 121-122, 124, 151, 161,
    181
Gitt, Josiah William 172
Goldman, Eric 178-179
Goldwater, Barry 134
Greenfield, Meg 46-47
Greenville, North Carolina 42

H

Hagerty, James 94
Hamilton, Alexander 50, 52
Harris, Survey 137, 179
Heath, Ted 32
Heiskell, John N. 173
Henry, Patrick 49, 51
Hitler, Adolf 178
Hohenberg, John 158-159
House of Commons 29, 108
Howard, Estella 141
Humphrey, Hubert H. 7-8, 42,
    113, 115
Huntley, Chet 62, 80, 157

I

Image 27-28, 31, 83-84; image
    building 30, 32; image capital
    9, 19-22, 29, 30-32

In-depth reporting—see Reporting
Indo-Chinese War 176

J

J. F. K. The Man and the Myth 47
Jackson, Andrew 52
Jackson, Justice Robert 109
Jackson, Mississippi 42-43
Jefferson, Thomas 51-52
John Birch Society 173
Johnson, Lyndon 20, 22-23, 29-30, 32, 39, 53-56, 65, 113, 132, 177-184; Administration 17
Journalistic Elite 46, 56

K

Kennedy, John Fitzgerald 20-23, 40-43, 47, 138; Administration 17
Kennedy, Robert F. 113, 132
Kerner Commission—see National Advisory Commission on Civil Disorders
Kerner, Otto 181
King, Martin Luther 183
Klein, Herbert G. 10, 32, 89-103; biography 91

L

Labour Party (Britain) 26
LaFollette, Robert 173
Lambert, Gerald 139-140
Lang, Gladys 145-67; biography 147-48
Lang, Kurt 145-67; biography 147-48
Lasky, Victor 46-47
Life 174
Lincoln, Abraham 52-53
Lippman, Theo 112
Lippmann, Walter 48, 56
Literary Digest 139

Little Rock Arkansas 173
Lobby correspondents (Britain) 24, 27-28
Lodge, Henry Cabot 41
Los Angeles, California 80, 122
Los Angeles Times 10, 48, 77, 79, 84, 121-23

M

MacArthur Day parade 149-50
MacArthur, Douglas 149
McCarthy, Joseph 109-110, 113, 173
McCarthy, Richard 66
McGinley, Phyllis 136
McGovern, George 69-70
McLuhan, Marshall 156
Macmillan, Harold 20, 23-28
Maddox, Lester 8
Madison (Wisconsin) *Capital Times* 173
Madison, James 50-51
Maryland, University of—Department of Journalism 9
Media controls 7
Memphis, Tennessee 42
Montgomery, Alabama 8
Morton, Thurston 43
Moyers, Bill 94
Muckraking 174
Murrow, Edward R. 25
Muskie, Edmund S. 112

N

National Advisory Commission on Civil Disorders (Kerner Commission) 126, 151, 161, 181-84
National conventions 113
National Security Council 95
New Delhi, India 115-116
New Republic 178-179
New York, New York 80

New York Times 7, 48, 61-62, 114
News: believability 101; bias 62, 65, 68, 81, 156; criteria 62; definitions 110, 125; distortion 60, 83, 125-26, 145-67; leak 68-70; management 17, 48, 52-53, 64-65, 70-71, 81 (also see selective disclosure); objectivity 61-63 (also see Reporting and Reporter); political bias 10, 57-74; reliability 85; selection 79, 115, 152, 166-67; selective disclosure 65-69; television networks 6, 151, 157
News magazines 81, 84, 174
Newspapers 81-84, 92, 101, 121, 123, 125, 137, 157, 162, 164-65, 173-74, 177, 184-86
Nixon, Richard 31-32, 40-42, 46-47, 56, 92, 100, 113-114, 175; Administration 8, 10, 68, 89-103
Nolan, Martin F. 115
No. 10 Downing 23-24, 29

O

Objectivity—see Reporting, objective
Oishi, Gene 112
Opinionmakers 99
Opinion Polls 11, 114-115, 129-143; accuracy 135; polling methods 133, 135; poll use 137-143

P

Parliament 97
Peace Corps 142
Pearl Harbor 177-178
Pentagon 69
Philadelphia, Pennsylvania 49
Pinckney, Cotesworth 50

Polls—see Opinion Polls
Potter, Philip 10, 105-116; biography 107
Power in Washington 108
Presidential politics 13-33; press conferences 21-22, 25, 32, 82, 96-97; press secretaries 94
Press Corps—see Reporters
Princeton University 11
Public Opinion Polls—see Opinion Polls
Public relations, use of 30

R

Radio 80, 92, 101, 125, 163, 166
Raspberry, William 11, 117-128; biography 119-120
Reagan, Ronald 83
Reid, Bishop James Madison 41-42
The Reporter 40
Reporter: news 82-84, 87, 92, 96-98, 112, 121, 150, 152, 154, 157-158, 165; objectivity 109, 152; political 113-116; press corps 24, 47, 111; selectivity 62, 79, 115, 152; skepticism 70-71; television 7, 151
Reporting: in depth 164, 166; objective 83, 115, 151-52; subjective 83
Republicans 39-41, 43, 54, 98, 109, 178, 182
Reston, James 48
Rioting 121-23, 151
Rivers, William L. 9, 35-55; biography 37
Robinson, Jackie 41-42
Rockefeller, Nelson 182
Roll, Charles 138
Romney, George 115, 132
Roosevelt, Franklin D. 26, 52, 54-55, 139, 177-178

Roosevelt, Theodore 52
Roper Poll 179
Rosten, Leo 111

S

St. Louis Post-Dispatch 185-86
Salinger, Pierre 94
Santa Barbara (California) *News-Press* 173
Schramm, Wilbur 39
Schwarz, Fred 44-46
Scott, Hugh 40-41, 43
Secrecy in Government 49
Selective Processes 10, 38-44, 56; selective exposure 39, 44; selective perception 39-43, 153; selective retention 39, 44
Selection criteria, political reporting 105-116
Sevareid, Eric 48, 80
Shapiro, Samuel 181
Smith, Ian 28
Storke, Thomas More 173
Supreme Court, United States 43, 109, 174

T

Taft, Robert 155
Technology, in Communication 11, 165-67
Television 6, 16, 22-23, 25, 27, 79-85, 87, 92, 96-97, 101, 125; television bias 153-154, 167; credibility 156, 161; demonstrations 153; distortion 145-167; documentary 163-164, 166; news 156; news management 154; pseudo events 68, 154-155
Television and Politics 149
Thurmond, Strom 68
Time 17, 44
Tory party (Britain) 26

The Tragedy of Lyndon Johnson 178
Trial balloon 70

U

United Press International 56
United Nations 41
Urban poor 11, 160

V

VISTA 142
Variety 115
Vietcong 100
Vietnam 8, 29, 68, 87, 92, 100, 132, 141, 163, 172, 174-175, 177
Volpe, John 182

W

Walker Report 151
Wall Street Journal 177
Wallace, George C. 112-113, 134
The Washington Evening Star 48
Washington, George 50, 52
Washington Monthly 114
Washington Post, The 11, 48, 62, 77, 114, 121-122,
Watts, California 121
White House 18, 23, 69, 95, 97, 179
Whiteford, Charles 112
Wilson, Harold 20, 26-30, 32
Wire services 110, 140

Y

York (Pennsylvania) *Gazette and Daily* 172
Yorty, Sam 83-84
Young, Whitney 124

Z

Ziegler, Ronald 32, 94